Kraushar, Peter Maximilian.
New products and diversification [by]
Peter M. Kraushar. 2nd ed. London,
Business Books, 1977.
x, 212 p. illus. 23 cm.

New Products and Diversification

Second Edition

NEW PRODUCTS AND DIVERSIFICATION

Peter M. Kraushar, MA(Cantab)

Chairman and Managing Director,
Kraushar Andrews & Eassie Limited
Managing Director, Pricing Research Limited
Chairman, Marketing Society, 1973-4, 1974-5

BUSINESS BOOKS LIMITED
Communica Europa
London

First published 1969
Second impression 1970
Second edition 1977

ISBN 0 220 66308 4

Printed in Great Britain by litho at The Anchor Press Ltd, and bound by Wm Brendon & Son Ltd, both of Tiptree, Essex

Contents

Introduction to the first edition

New product development and diversification are subjects which are now recognised to be vital to the future of companies. The government, too, have realised the importance of general innovation by industry at large and its effects on the competitiveness of UK industry in world markets.

I have also found that these are fascinating subjects in which every executive is very interested and generally holds strong views. The very mention of development is enough to start a discussion on why some new products fail and others succeed, the best organisation for development, etc.

Yet whenever I am asked to recommend a book on the subject which deals specifically with UK experience, I am always at a loss, because as far as I know no such book exists. I have dared to put pen to paper, therefore, in an attempt to satisfy this market gap.

I have tried to draw as much as possible on my experience of over 300 projects, because I believe that in development and diversification, as in many aspects of business, there is a strong divergence between theory and practice and it is useless to draw up very sophisticated models or complicated mathematical 'solutions' if no one can understand them or has the time to use them. For example, a mathematical approach to development, though it had achieved some success in the United States, failed to find a single buyer in the UK, because a company's management did not have enough faith to be guided in important investment decisions by an answer given by a computer at the end of a process which only an experienced mathematician could begin to understand. Who can blame the management for not trying?

At the same time, I have resisted the temptation of looking at all the projects I have worked on, in order to derive some statistical data from them. One of the main lessons I have learned about development lies in the differences rather than the similarities between companies, so statistics can be misleading and I have tried to use the experience in a qualitative sense instead.

It would be unrealistic to expect that such a book can provide answers to specific development problems. There is no magic formula to success in development and each individual or each company concerned will need to find its own path to that goal. I hope, however, that this book will provide general information to all those interested in the topic and a background to those actually involved in this field which they will be able to adapt to their own circumstances. It should also be particularly suitable to advanced students of marketing and of business in general.

In many cases the reader may feel that I am simply stating the obvious. If this is so, I apologise, but my excuse is that so often even large and sophisticated companies are terribly inefficient in development and diversification and the most obvious points are rarely put into practice.

I have concentrated on consumer rather than on industrial goods because my experience is mainly with the former. Much of the approach can be adapted for industrial goods, but I do not believe that the two categories can be covered satisfactorily in one book.

My thanks to the companies and to my colleagues with whom I have discussed every aspect of development and diversification over many years. And to the Baker Library at Harvard for having such a splendid collection of US books on marketing subjects, of which I availed myself while on an International Marketing Institute course there. Finally, I must thank my wife to whom this book is dedicated. Over the last year she must have thought that she had married a book rather than a husband.

London, March 1970

Introduction to the second edition

I first wrote this book in the late 1960s because I felt that the subject of new product development and diversification was important and companies had hardly become expert in this area, as shown by the frequent new product failures experienced by even major companies. Moreover there were no books in the UK covering the subject in any depth, while the US books were strangely unsatisfactory.

In the last seven years many books have been written on new products and countless launches have taken place, but I wish that one could state that the success rate has much improved; unfortunately there is no certain sign of this, although methods have become more sophisticated.

I must have now worked on over 1000 development projects of various kinds and hope that I have learnt something in the process. I certainly believe that, as so often, there is no substitute for experience in this area and despair when I see the absurd results of theory unsupported by practical knowledge. This new edition is considerably changed in the light of another seven years of continuous practice; although there is no magic formula for success, I hope that the reader will adapt my conclusions to his own needs.

London, October 1976

1 The need for new products or for diversification

Definition

The term 'new product' can cover a multitude of sins:

1 Small changes to an existing brand such as new packaging, new sizes or the addition of new varieties.
2 Major innovations in a company's existing markets.
3 A product similar or identical to one already being marketed by a competitor, but in a market new to the company concerned.
4 A product different from any being marketed in the same country, but already existing abroad.
5 A product which is different from any marketed by anyone anywhere, i.e. a true innovation.

My own definition covers categories 2, 3, 4, and 5 above. Moreover it includes new products which a company obtains from acquisition, as well as those resulting from Research and Development activity within the company. Acquisitions are normally treated separately from new product development, but there is a close connection between the two approaches to innovation or diversification, so it is important to look at both together.

Awareness of need

Even a few years ago, certainly in the early 1950s, many companies did not think that new products were necessary to them. Their growth had been based often on one or two products which had perhaps played a predominant role in the company's history, e.g. sugar for Tate and Lyle, tea for Brooke Bond, chocolate for Cadbury's, stout for Guinness, bicycles for Raleigh, and it did not seem to make sense that a satisfactory profit position should be jeopardised by going in for new things, often in fields in which the company would have little or no experience.

Since then, however, the situation has changed completely. In the late 1950s and early 1960s the importance of new products became recognised to such an extent that it is never challenged today. In fact it is difficult to find recent quotations on this matter, probably because it is now felt that they would be no more than platitudes, repeating an established fact.

Some of the earlier statements were interesting. In 1960 a Nielsen survey showed that in the United States 47 per cent of fast-moving consumer goods audited by them represented brands launched since 1950. In 1964 the Deputy Chairman of the UK Campbell Soup Company estimated that by 1974 up to 80 per cent of grocery trade turnover would come from new products not existing at the time. Also in 1964 Nielsen reported that over half of consumer spending on packaged detergents was on products launched after 1950. In France it was estimated by Leduc (1966) [1.1] that 73 per cent of the detergent market was held by brands launched in the previous 8 years. In 1965 J. Walter Thompson [1.2] analysed a sample of UK product categories from grocery price lists between 1954 and 1964. It was estimated that of the 534 company names listed in 1964 in the 29 categories covered over half had entered these fields since 1954. Prof. Pessemier [1.3] estimates that in 1965 3 per cent of the gross national product (GNP) was devoted in the United States to the development of new products and services – more than double the expenditure in 1957. R&D expenditure in the UK had similarly shot up.

This trend changed recently, however, and even in the United States R&D expenditure was no higher in real terms in 1973 than in 1969. This reflects the realisation that fundamental research may not pay off in product terms and is best left to government and universities. Applied research and interest in new products continue to be at a very high level, however.

The case for innovation seems proved and nearly every company accepts it. Brooke Bond have diversified into coffee, food broking, cheese, spices, meat and even paperbacks. Tate and Lyle announced in December 1967 the formation of a new company for diversification and in 1974 sugar accounted for only a quarter of their business. Guinness have moved into lager, plastics, confectionery and leisure. I have discussed personally the matter of innovation with over five hundred consumer goods companies in the period 1966-76 and not one challenged the need for new products.

Perhaps the best proof of their need is the continuation of new product activity in 1975-6 – both in Europe and in North America – although the economic situation and the high interest rates might be expected to stop most companies. I obtained clear evidence in the UK that the 1975 economic chaos has in no way stopped new product activity by packaged goods companies. I carried out a survey among 90 such companies in April 1975 [1.4] with results shown in Table 1.1. These results clearly show that, even in extremely difficult times, the majority of companies keep their new product development programme and indeed many even increase it and plan more launches than before; the problems on current brands coupled with uncertainties for the future make even

TABLE 1.1

Current size of new product development programme compared with average for previous three years	Larger	36
	Same	33
	Smaller	21
		90
Doing more or less new product research to cut down risks	More	38
	Same	46
	Less	6
		90
Planning more or less launches than before in 1975/6	More	39
	Same	28
	Less	22
	n/a	1
		90

 large established products less secure than before and lead companies to try to spread their risks by broadening the base.

Product life cycles – a useful idea?

Nielsen [1.5] recently produced some useful evidence on the life cycles of new products, based on the investigation of 454 grocery brands from 35 product categories in the United States and from 39 product categories in Britain during the period 1961-66. Nielsen defined as a brand's primary cycle the period from a brand's initial growth up to the time when its share fell below 80 per cent of the first crest. On this basis 54 per cent of the new brands had a primary cycle lasting under two years and only 13 per cent continued to grow after three years.

The US section of the study also clearly showed the expected decrease in the length of the primary cycle as markets have become increasingly competitive over the years. In the product categories covered the median length of primary cycles was three years in 1962 and only 18 months in 1964.

Finally an important number of brands were subjected to a recycle following the primary cycle, i.e. strong marketing action was taken once the brands had been shown to decline, and 40 per cent of the recycles included product innovation. It is noteworthy, however, that the average length of a recycle was only fifteen months and was becoming shorter each succeeding year covered by the study.

The above findings clearly illustrate how terrifyingly short a product's life cycle is becoming, certainly in the case of recently introduced products, though it must be borne in mind that this aspect would have been exaggerated by Nielsen's concentration on fast-moving grocery products.

It is also to be noted that the Nielsen data apply only to products introduced recently. It is possible and indeed it is likely that the life cycle of a new product these days is very short and is becoming shorter all the time, whereas the picture is very different in the case of the old-established products. If this is so, it is an important point closely related to the need for new products in companies which possess some old-established ones.

For example, there is no sign that products such as Bisto, Bovril, Guinness, Dettol, Horlicks, Ovaltine and many others of this vintage are declining or dying. Whatever should be happening to them on a life-cycle basis, these products are not only alive but they are prospering and in general increasing turnover and profits over the years.

It is easy to be frightened regarding the future of a company's products even if they are healthy and prospering. For example, Theodore Levitt's famous article 'Marketing myopia' [1.6] had a salutary effect when first published in showing how companies do not innovate in their own fields through having too narrow a view of them – the US railways should have thought that they were not in rail but in transport and so should have gone into air transport – but this argument is now used to persuade companies to diversify at all cost. Yet timing is vital and there is certainly some evidence that companies should not be too pessimistic regarding the time-span within which an old-established product will continue to be profitable.

Moreover, I believe that there is considerable room for improvement in extending life cycles if the company plans accordingly. For example, if it is accepted that a new product will be declining after, say, three years and nothing is done until the decline sets in, the company deserves the failure it probably has on its hands. If, on the other hand, this factor is taken into account before the product is launched, it may be possible to build ingredients into the product and its marketing which will allow it to extend its cycle at the critical points. Thus the profit pattern can be transformed from the pattern shown in Figure 1.1*a* to that in Figure 1.1*b*.

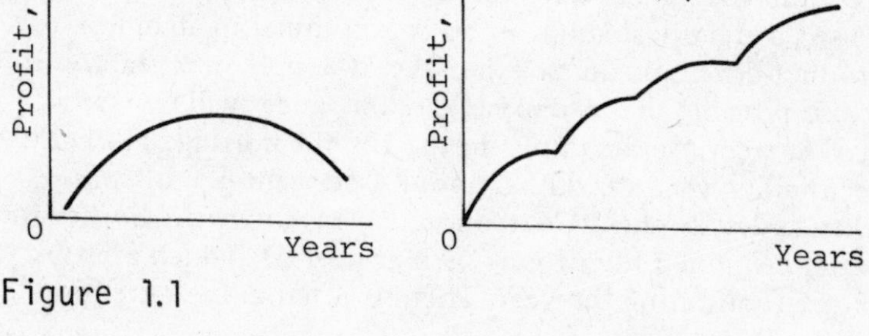

Figure 1.1

Such cycle extension may sound highly theoretical, but in fact has taken place a number of times and Theodore Levitt [1.7] has described three successful cases – Nylon, General Foods' Jell-O and Minnesota Mining and Manufacturing Company's 'Scotch' Tape. In all three cases the companies had planned an extension of either the product's number of users or of its actual uses at critical points. In practice on a number of occasions, when the growth pattern was beginning to fail, the companies were completely successful in putting their plans in operation.

In the case of nylon, Du Pont extended its use first into other types of hosiery – highly patterned and coloured stockings – and then into new product categories such as carpets, tyres, etc. Similarly, Jell-O extended its cycle first by adding new varieties, then by extending its uses to salads and finally by finding new users – weight watchers – and by finding completely new uses for the basic gelatine.

It is this kind of planning which can make the difference between success and relative failure. Nylon is still going strong but, as Levitt says, this would not have happened if new uses had not been found for the same basic material. There were danger points in its growth in 1945, 1948, 1955 and 1959 and decline could well have set in at these points, but each time Du Pont had a trick up its sleeve.

The development and redevelopment of nylon illustrates what can often be done in the case of many products and services. In fact I wonder whether the idea of a life cycle serves a really useful purpose because it is too easy to give up a product as approaching the end of its cycle, whereas a businessman unbothered by marketing theory would just think that the product is in trouble and would fight hard to halt the decline. After all the old product is already in production, has a certain consumer and trade franchise, and the company knows a great deal about it. So it is criminal to abandon 'old product development' for the sake of a marketing theory. It is also possible that economic circumstances will reverse a market trend; for example, in the UK the porridge market had been falling very steadily at about 4 per cent p.a. in volume when suddenly the 1974 economic crisis drove the housewife to old fashioned filler foods such as porridge which grew by 15 per cent during the year. There is often more hope for old products than the marketing man will admit.

Nevertheless, it seems reasonable to believe that products finally really do decline and die and companies need to plan continually to develop new products to add to and eventually to supersede the existing ones, so long as the life cycle idea is treated with caution.

But are new products automatic salvation?

An existing product must eventually die. The rate of change is accelerating. Life cycles are becoming shorter and shorter. A company's salvation must lie in new products. The case seems proved.

Yet in real life the situation is not so simple. The importance of new products is so well known now in most companies that this thinking has actually become dangerous to many, because new products have become manna from heaven, the answer to every problem. This attitude can lead to a new disease, 'new product hysteria', resulting in quick acquisitions or new product launches which, if unsuccessful, can inhibit the company's progress for a long time, not only in financial terms but also by putting up psychological barriers against future innovation. How many companies there are with such a go/stop policy, launching in too much of a hurry and then being afraid of doing anything else for ten years!

If I sound over-pessimistic, let us look at some facts. How many successes have been launched in the UK in the last ten years? Although no exact figures are available, there are some useful indications. William Ramsay, Development Manager of Alfred Bird (now General Foods) looked in April 1967 [1.8] at major grocery brands launched in the UK in the period 1956-65. He classified these as having annual sales of at least £1 million at retail selling price (RSP) and on the basis of Nielsen data estimated that only 25 products launched since 1956 had achieved the £1 million mark. These only represented between 15 per cent and 20 per cent of all grocery products retailing at over £1 million.

A more recent study [1.9] covered new packaged food products launched since 1959 and produced the pattern shown in Figure 1.2; It can be seen that there has been an

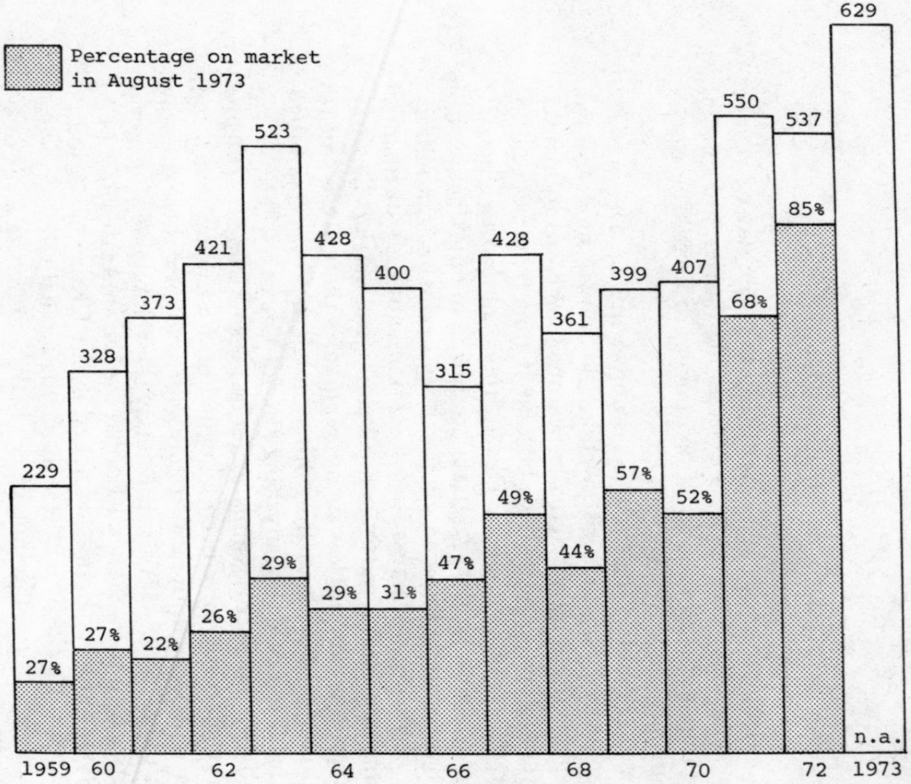

Figure 1.2 Packaged food products launched and percentage on market in August 1973

increasing number of new products in the categories covered – rising from 229 in 1959 to 629 in 1973 – but the large majority of those launched before 1966 are no longer on the shelves and it can be assumed that others have not been withdrawn but have not been successful. It is in the grocery markets that sophisticated new product development and research have taken place. Large grocery companies tend to have specialist departments concentrating on new product development; market research budgets exceeding £100,000 p.a. are common; discounted cash flow, net work analysis, modelling have all become standard procedures in many companies; yet there is hardly a large company without a hideous skeleton in its cupboard of new product failures. Certainly new products are not the automatic solution to every problem. The figures above surely deserve much reflection.

What about acquisitions? How have they fared? Here it is even more difficult to give a definite answer, but there are again indications that many are unsuccessful (see page 190). This view is supported by a study conducted in the United Stated by John Kitching [1.10], who later carried out similar studies in Europe. He covered the acquisition policy of 20 US companies and examined in detail 69 acquisitions which they had made at least two years before the survey. Nineteen were considered failures and three others were considered failures at first, but were later turned into successes. In general he felt that the top executives interviewed were unhappy about their companies' acquisition activities, being particularly uneasy about the high degree of risk involved which was so difficult to quantify when compared with other forms of investment. Likewise, 20-30 per cent of the European acquisitions were unqualified failures.

In my experience, the findings described above certainly apply to the UK to an even greater extent, because there is no doubt that US companies are ahead in sophisticated techniques designed to appraise acquisitions. Moreover, at last it is recognised that size does not necessarily lead to success.

If, however, it is so difficult to innovate or diversify, is it better not to try? Have the arguments advanced earlier in this book gone overboard? The answer is no, definitely not. I draw four main conclusions:

1 Companies must have a balanced attitude towards new products and acquisitions. They must not regard them as automatic solutions to their problems. It is important, therefore, that every effort be made to optimise first the results from the company's existing products so that, if the company decides to embark on the uncharted waters of innovation or diversification, it does so with a solid, well-manned ship.

2 Innovation need not be the most profitable course for every company. It is possible that in some cases the shareholders' interests are best served, certainly in the short and medium term, by a conscious decision to concentrate on the existing products without any innovation apart from minor product improvements.

3 In the long term, however, a company's future must lie in innovation. Otherwise, however good its products, it will be caught out by the competition just as Henry Ford was caught by General Motors because of his persistence with his Model T.

A company should certainly seek new products, but this should be done with a real understanding of the risks involved. It is necessary, therefore, for a company to adopt an organisation, a set of procedures and an attitude of mind which are appropriate to the opportunities and the risks presented by new products.

The need for new products is very real, but the need to understand the implications is as important.

4 Innovation must not be confused with diversification. Companies can be most successful by limiting their operations to a very restricted field, so long as they are prepared to innovate in order to defend their long-term future in that field. For example, it is believed that Wrigley's policy is to restrict themselves to chewing gum, in which they are dominant internationally, and this approach has been very successful and profitable.

Diversification into new fields probably presents greater opportunities, but also has far greater risks. The decision whether a company should diversify or just innovate in its current fields is probably the most important one that it needs to take and the relative advantages and disadvantages of the two approaches deserve very detailed examination. In my experience this rarely happens.

Some company histories

It is instructive to look at a number of companies in relation to their new product development and diversification activities.

(a) Robertson Foods

The company is an old established UK manufacturer traditionally dominant in the static jam and marmalade market. With a turnover of £46 million in 1975-6 it is almost unique in its position as a branded food manufacturer which has not been swallowed up by a major group, so its development has had to be relatively modest on a scale appropriate to the size of the company.

Sales and profits are given in Table 1.2 and show the problems facing a medium-sized food company in the UK in the

TABLE 1.2

Year ending 31 March	Sales, £m	Profits before tax, £m	Return on capital employed, %
1965	14.1	1.0	19
1966	15.3	1.2	20
1967	16.0	1.3	20
1968	17.7	1.5	22
1969	17.7	1.3	18
1970	17.7	1.1	14
1971	19.6	1.1	13
1972	23.6	1.7	17
1973	26.5	2.0	18
1974	32.8	1.9	17
1975	41.8	2.1	19
1976	45.9	2.3	19

1960s and 1970s. In the mid-1960s Robertsons were enjoying a return on capital of around 20 per cent on static turnover, depending almost entirely on preserves. New products, such as an attempt to enter the fiercely competitive fruit squash market, were unsuccessful, though modest turnover was achieved through launch of Robertsons Fruit Fillings, a new market being developed in 1964-5.

Then the company began to stir; Viota was bought and so Robertson diversified into cake mixes and private label breakfast cereals; British Canners were bought giving Robertsons production facilities for canned fruit and vegetables; finally Peny SA was bought in France giving Robertsons a foothold in Europe in canned vegetables and prepared meals. Thus by 1975/6 only 58 per cent of turnover was in preserves, 20 per cent in canned fruit and vegetables, 9 per cent in cake mixes, 11 per cent in breakfast cereals and 3 per cent in other products.

The company has developed almost entirely by acquisition and almost doubled profit before tax by doing so, though without allowance for inflation. Return on capital has dropped, however, but has improved recently and the company has done extremely well to raise it in the difficult years of 1974-6.

(b) *Marks and Spencer*

There is no need to describe what is one of the best known retailing operations in the world. What is interesting is that its development has relied relatively little on new stores or on acquisitions; it has been largely based on continuously improved use of its selling area as shown in Table 1.3. These figures reflect the achievement of Marks and Spencer. Over 12 years turnover has gone up 330 per cent while sales area increased by only 76 per cent, reflecting very steady growth in sales per square foot, though in the last three years increases have been due to inflation. Even more noteworthy has been maintenance of the unusually high 13 per cent margin till the inevitable fall recently. The company has built this profitability on the basis of clothing and other textiles and food being retailed as good quality and value but not necessarily low cost items. Many believe that its major development has

TABLE 1.3

Year ending 31 March	Sales, £m	Profits before tax, £m	Sales area, '000 ft^2	£ sales per sq. ft	Profits as % of sales
1965*	209	27.5	3337	6	13
1966	226	29.6	3471	6	13
1967	243	30.7	3635	7	13
1968	269	33.9	3929	7	13
1969	300	38.1	4214	7	13
1970	339	43.7	4408	8	13
1971*	391	50.1	4708	8	13
1972	439	53.8	4944	9	12
1973	522	70.0	5059	10	13
1974	605	76.8	5489	11	13
1975	722	81.9	5712	13	11
1976*	901	83.6	5868	15	9

*53 weeks

been into food retailing, but food in fact represented an important proportion of sales long before the war. It is certainly interesting that in the traditionally low margin food area (it accounted for 30 per cent of sales in 1975/6 – as much as women's outerwear), margins have been high because of the policy of providing high quality and relatively high price food, many of the products being available in Marks and Spencer only.

This company shows what can be done by constant development and improvement in one's current operation rather than by 'blue sky' diversification. The main development for the future will probably be in attempts to repeat the same formula abroad, initially in Canada, France and Benelux, again a safer formula for development than search for many new areas in the UK.

(c) *Reed International*

By contrast Reed International reflects a company, originally in the problem area of paper and board only, that decided to diversify from that base to spread the risk. Its record has been as shown in Table 1.4.

TABLE 1.4

Year ending 31 March	Sales, £m	Profit before tax, £m	Return on capital employed, %
1965	149	13.3	9
1966	226	19.4	8
1967	240	13.6	5
1968	250	14.2	6
1969	282	16.9	6
1970	314	19.3	7
1971	502	19.9	5
1972	534	30.1	7
1973	598	42.6	9
1974	734	65.5	12
1975	969	85.4	14

The group has grown largely by acquisitions, the largest being of Wall Paper Manufacturers and of IPC, but considerable development has taken place in the various divisions; for example the launch of Crown Plus Two Paint by WPM has probably been the most successful paint launch in the DIY market and has carved out a major share for Reed.

Even so the figures show that the problems have not been solved entirely. The group is, of course, on a much more diversified base than ever before and has even managed to raise its return on capital; it is still low, however, at only 14 per cent and it remains to be seen whether the wide base now achieved can be developed profitably; only then will the last few years' growth policy be completely vindicated.

(d) Imperial Group

Imperial decided, like Reed, to diversify from its current operation concentrated entirely on tobacco. The difference was the very high returns in tobacco which were most unlikely to be generated in other areas. Its development away from tobacco is shown in Table 1.5.

By 1974/5 the group has become very diversified, the

TABLE 1.5

Year ending 31 October	Sales, £m	Profit before tax, £m	Return on capital employed, %
1965	796	37.3	9
1966	908	44.4	11
1967	946	47.5	10
1968	1015	54.7	10
1969	1126	56.5	10
1970	1272	61.5	11
1971	1276	68.2	11
1972	1361	78.5	10
1973	1584	97.3	9
1974	1879	73.5	7
1975	2354	106.8	9

tobacco turnover being artificially exaggerated by the very large proportion of duty. Tobacco still accounted for 57 per cent of profits, but brewing (through acquisition of Courage) had 21 per cent, paper, board and packaging (Mardon 50 per cent owned, Albion Bottle, etc.) 5 per cent, food (Golden Wonder, Ross, Smedley HP) 15 per cent. Even so yet again the diversification has had a serious effect on the company's profitability, though in the long term it must be right to diversify from tobacco. The problems of diversifying into new areas large enough to make any difference to Imperial and yet profitable enough not to dilute too much the tobacco profitability must have been immense and, as so often happens, it is the original 'problem' area, i.e. tobacco which has propped up the operation by not declining in either turnover or profitability.

(e) Wrigley

I have chosen as a contrast a relatively small international company, Wm. Wrigley Jr Company, Chicago, which has made its name in one area – chewing gum – and which has no intention of departing from chewing gum. As the world becomes wealthier, people become more anxious and so are more likely to chew gum in the long term, so the future is favourable and one company has decided to become a major force in chewing gum internationally. The results of this policy have been as shown in Table 1.6.

Here is a company which up to 1973 has been achieving

TABLE 1.6

Calendar year	Sales, $m	Profit before tax, $m	Percentage on stockholders' equity
1970	177	29.7	26
1971	190	34.0	28
1972	207	35.3	27
1973	232	37.9	28
1974	272	34.0	24

TABLE 1.7

Year ending 30 Sept	Turnover, $m					Profit before tax, $m				
	Total	Agri-cul-ture	Con-sumer	Inter-national	Rest-aurant	Total	Agri-cul-ture	Con-sumer	Inter-national	Rest-aurant
1970	1417	733	321	293	69	146	69	47	18	12
1971	1592	739	395	332	111	156	63	60	19	14
1972	1774	754	475	441	145	162	45	74	24	19
1973	2434	1028	661	593	191	194	69	78	25	23
1974	3073	1296	836	672	269	226	79	89	28	50

excellent returns in its one chosen area. The 1974 fall was blamed on increasing sugar and labour costs. Over the years Wrigley's profits justified their policy and it is unlikely that diversification could solve the current short-term problems. So long as there is no ambition to become very much larger, there is perfect reason in running a profitable small operation which devotes itself to development of new chewing gum flavours, to optimisation of its current operation and for whom a very major development has been the launch of Freedent, the new chewing gum for people with false teeth.

The one problem which I can see in the Wrigley policy, so long as the long-term future for chewing gum is good, is that it does not provide much scope for ambitious executives in the company; normally a 'young tiger' in a company can see chances for his own development in new ventures; when the company decides to stay in chewing gum, the number of rewarding posts must be strictly limited.

(f) Ralston Purina

A US agricultural products company operating particularly in animal feeds, Ralston Purina have been diversifying into new areas. It has become a very large force in dry dog and cat food and has developed related consumer products – tuna, savoury snacks, breakfast cereals. In addition Ralston Purina have entered the area of fast foods and restaurants, as so many other US food manufacturers have done.

The figures in Table 1.7 show how the consumer division has become the company's biggest profit earner, reflecting particularly the performance of its petfoods, and in 1974/75 was forecast to provide almost twice as much profit as agriculture.

By September 1974 Ralston Purina had 787 'Jack in the Box' fast food restaurants and also 50 up-market conventional restaurants.

As a result of its agricultural operations, the company has become very involved in soya protein and developments in this area could show promise for the future.

Ralston Purina seems a good example of growth through development into areas related to its original base which have spread its operation both in the US and internationally.

2 New product failures

Rate of failures

Some new products fail and some succeed. But what is failure? What is success? How many fail? How many succeed? Why?

There are no satisfactory answers to the above questions, mainly because yet again the problem of definition is intractable. Not only is there the usual difficulty in defining a new product – every one uses different definitions – but also what would be a failure to one company could be a success to another. Moreover failure rate figures are applied to products in various stages of development. Some talk in terms of the percentage of new ideas which lead to one success. Others estimate the failure rate of products placed into test market.

It follows, therefore, that the wealth of information which exists on the failure rate of new products needs to be treated with care. The Shering Drug Company of New Jersey, for example, estimated in 1966 that they had screened 13,500 antibiotics during the previous year. Of these, 350 looked active and 16 seemed worth looking at, being different from existing products. Finally five were shortlisted and the company believed that one of them had a 33 per cent chance of being marketed. N. H. Borden, Jr [2.10, quoted in his doctoral thesis various estimates on the proportion of new items offered to US supermarkets which had in fact been accepted. A buyer from American Stores had estimated the figure at 977 out of 4303. Allied Supermarkets had considered 3696 new items over a twelve-month period and had accepted 756. In addition, many others had not been considered. *Progressive Grocer* estimated that 6000 new items had been offered to a typical US supermarket during 1961 and about 300 had been accepted.

In 1955 the New Product Institute Incorporated published the results of research among 200 large manufacturers of packaged consumer items in the United States who had introduced new products since 1945. All the companies were extremely successful and prosperous and had large resources to support the development and launch of new products. Yet, when asked about the success rate of new product launches, these 200 companies claimed that only 19 per cent of the products placed on the market in the previous few years had been successful. The majority (77 per cent) also claimed that their competitors had been even less successful, although one cannot imagine that bias would be absent from such an answer!

A more recent US survey [2.2] by the National Industrial Conference Board among major consumer goods companies suggested a more optimistic failure rate of only 40 per cent.

In the UK an analysis by Nielsen [2.3] of 44 new grocery products test marketed over a period of 14 years showed that almost half went on to national marketing, a similar proportion to that found by Nielsen in the US in 1962. The 1974 Kraushar, Andrews & Eassie study already mentioned [1.9] found that half the products launched in 1970 or before were no longer on the shelves by August 1973. By August 1975 it was only 41 per cent [2.4]. Other studies among the most successful packaged goods companies in the UK have suggested that a 50 per cent success rate is regarded as very good indeed.

It seems pointless, in my opinion, to explore the failure rate further because it is impossible to establish an accurate figure and it does not matter whether the rate of 90 per cent, 80 per cent or even 70 per cent. What is important is to establish certain general conclusions:

1. A very large number of new product ideas are necessary at the initial stage for weeding out through subsequent stages if a successful product is to be achieved at the end of the process.
2. Even when a new product is produced and marketed, a large proportion fail – well over half. I am convinced that the Nielsen failure rate after test market is an underestimate for two main reasons:
   - *(a)* The companies using Nielsen tend to be above average in marketing expertise and so are likely to do much more pre-testing than the average company.
   - *(b)* It is not possible to define a success or failure accurately without knowledge of the profit figures.

> It is common to see companies launching new products after test market though the test market indicates failure. Alternatively a product successful in test market may for various reasons become unprofitable in national marketing. Yet any product launched nationally after test market would have been included by Nielsen in the successful category.

It should be accepted, therefore, that new product development is a hazardous business, whatever the failure rate. What is more rewarding and useful than study of the failure rate is analysis of actual failures to establish whether there are any general principles which can be applied.

Some failures

A study of product failures over the last fifteen years shows that a very large number have taken place, although it is difficult to obtain information about them as most companies are keener to shout about their successes than about their failures.

The Edsel disaster in the United States, despite Ford's meticulous research programme, is very well known. In fact, almost every important consumer goods manufacturer, however experienced and sophisticated in marketing methods, has one or more skeletons locked in the new product disaster cupboard.

Unilever, for example, lost a great deal of money in launching Spree – a squash concentrate packed in small sachets. There seemed to be little demand for the product at a price which was very high in relation to the usual squash bottle.

ICI recently launched a range of do-it-yourself products designed to break into the Polycell franchise in this field, which seem to have met with little success despite the considerable effort put behind this venture, as the products had no important consumer advantage.

Polycell equally had had its failures. For example, an interesting venture into boats failed mainly because in practice the distribution side proved too much of a problem, i.e. there were no suitable retail outlets on a national basis. Beechams too has had its failures. For example, it developed a shampoo with a new method of application which was launched nationally after a seemingly successful test market; initial success was only due to a high trial rate but the fall was very rapid as the novelty wore off and the public returned to conventional products. More recently Beechams, Bristol Myers and others all launched men's hair sprays, spending very heavily on advertising in a tiny market which proved to have insufficient growth potential. Ready meals have been a real graveyard for new products. The large potential for a convenience meals has attracted almost every food company. Crosse and Blackwell, Cadbury Schweppes, Heinz, Colman's, Pillsbury, CPC, all had dismal failures, the most recent one of skillet meals being particularly horrific. Yet, possibly with hindsight, it can be seen that housewives showed their intelligence in not accepting products which tended to be expensive and of minority appeal, often selling in a combined pack products which the housewife could buy separately much more cheaply. Likewise kit desserts such as Batchelor's Promise failed because housewives felt that they were paying for a pretty carton. In a completely different area Allied Ironfounders launched a new bath in the UK and based their planning and product design entirely on US findings. The launch was not a success for the simple reason that Americans consider a bath very differently from Britons.

There have been several interesting cases of two or more companies launching similar products and meeting with very different results. A good example was the launch of Frutips by Nestlé, a range of chewy sweets which was almost the same as Opal Fruits launched by Mars at the same time. Opal Fruits went on to be one of the more successful new confectionery lines whereas Frutips soon failed. Why? The main difference was not between the products – both were very acceptable to the public – or between the marketing methods. I believe that the main difference lay in the suitability of the market for the two companies. Mars was very much more of a 'sweet' company than Nestlé from the point of view of both the trade and the public and had previously introduced other successful lines. Therefore, other things being equal, it was much easier for Mars than for Nestlé to launch such a product. Likewise it would have been much more difficult for Mars to launch a tinned cream product than it was for Nestlé, whose Nestlé's

Cream has been one of the more successful food products in the UK after the war.

The chocolate and sugar confectionery market has in fact been one of the most difficult ones for new products. There is some similarity with the shampoo market as here again the consumer seeks variety and is very happy to try new products, but is rarely satisfied with them for long. Thus the market is mostly dominated by lines which have been in existence for many years despite all the efforts at innovation by the main manufacturers. A good example of a promising new line was Mackintosh's Caramac, a chocolate bar which achieved immediate success until the public became weary of it. More recently, Cadburys launched a bevy of products in 1973 and, after initial success, most have declined steadily.

The slimming remedy market has been another where products have been launched with high hopes, to be quashed as the public refused to continue to buy the products regularly. Largely on the basis of US trends it was expected that this market would become very large, but this has not happened and Mead Johnson's Metercal was only one of a score of such products which were extremely disappointing. The UK launch of instant breakfast products that had been successful in the US also met with disaster – not surprising, as the surprised British public were asked to drink strawberry and raspberry drinks, based on synthetic chemicals, at breakfast! The concept could still work if adapted to British tastes.

Timing is clearly an important factor, and yet it is so difficult to judge in advance whether a product is too early for its market or not. Malling [2.5] quotes the Chrysler Airflow design of 1934 as 8-10 years too early. The Edsel's failure was probably due to bad timing. General Electric marketed the 'V' wire-wound resistor which was hailed by everyone at first and was a terrible failure – it was too late.

Similarly CPC test-marketed in the UK the fabric softener, Nu Soft, in the early 1960s and had to withdraw it, although fabric softeners had become very popular in the US by then. Lever Brothers subsequently spent a great deal of money 'educating' the British housewives to buy their softener, Comfort, until 1973 when Colgate launched Softlan followed by Procter and Gamble's Lenor. The market has suddenly exploded and it is by no means certain that the pioneers, Levers, will obtain their due reward; Colgate and Procter and Gamble may well enjoy the benefit (or luck) of accurate timing.

In the UK Birds Eye has tried to launch frozen orange juice a number of times and each time results have been disappointing because we are still far behind the US in our breakfast habits and in our possession of refrigerators and freezers. It may be a success in a few years' time. Nestea was an important failure for Nestlé despite the very large expenditure behind it. Both Cadburys and Batchelors also tried to launch instant tea and both failed too. The failures were mainly attributed to the British teamaking ritual, yet this has now been disturbed by tea bags and instant tea may well be acceptable in the years to come if the products are improved.

Instant potato products are a good example of different rates of acceptance due to timing. In the early 1960s Bibby, Batchelor and Mars tested instant potato products with considerable backing, but the results were poor. Since then the market has slowly expanded until the late 1960s, when Mars launched a second product to complement its existing brand. Cadbury's entered the market, so did Ranks Hovis McDougall, though they later withdrew. So Cadbury's Smash and Mars Wondermash became large brands and everyone else looked on with interest at a very fast-expanding market which suddenly had become completely different from that a few years before.

Dishwashers are yet another category which has been disappointing in the UK so far, mainly because of bad timing. Over the last ten years it has been often said that the breakthrough would come and that, as the household's needs are becoming satisfied, the dishwasher would be the next appliance to turn to. This has certainly not happened so far, probably because of the repeated restrictions which consumer expenditure has been suffering. Even though Hoover launched a model in the late 1960s, household ownership in 1975 is still under 2 per cent.

It seems likely, however, that this is one of the appliances of the future and it is not surprising that most appliance manufacturers have a model ready to launch when the time is ripe.

Price in relation to the product has often been the cause of failure. A number of aerosol products have failed badly, e.g. aerosol shoe polishes, because the extra convenience has not outweighed the high price. The failure of Whoosh, the chocolate milk drink in an aerosol, can again be attributed to this reason, whereas on the other hand aerosol hair sprays have been a great success because a woman obviously thinks it is worth paying for the convenience of an aerosol in this case.

Harvey's of Bristol probably found an important opportunity in the launch of a range of branded wines to be distributed nationally under the name of Club No. 1. Unfortunately the price at which it was marketed was too high for the mass market seeking the reassurance of a national brand and they continued to drink the cheaper wines, however inferior. The opportunity in branded wines has been confirmed by the success of branded Mateus and by the later success of the major brewery groups in this market sector, e.g. Bass Charrington's Hirondelle.

Procter and Gamble's Cheer was another product to bite the dust because of price. A detergent with a duster enclosed in each pack, it was priced above other detergents and housewives showed that the higher price did not compensate for all the dusters. Kayser Bondor's venture into children's clothes met a similar fate. They were expensive, though of high quality, and did not meet the mother's demand for low-priced clothes for children who wear out their clothes so fast.

Failure may stem from prices that are too low as well as from those that are too high. I know of at least two products launched by very large companies at an incorrect price, so that the more that was sold the greater the loss. Not surprisingly, they were both withdrawn. Pricing was also a factor in the staggering success and in the equally staggering failure of Rolls washing machines. The very low prices meant that extremely high turnover and tight financial control were essential for success. When the turnover fell and the financial control seemingly was not as tight as it might have been, failure was inevitable. The failure of Court Line in inclusive holidays, after initial success, was due to very much the same causes.

Many failures can be attributed to one general reason, i.e. to a wrong product. Either the product does not perform adequately or it is not significantly different from existing products or, even if it is different, there is no dissatisfaction with existing products which would lead the public to switch to a new product. Thus General Mills' Betty Crocker cake mixes were a complete failure in the UK because the products were unsuitable for the British market. Equally, Colmans had product problems with Toasty Grills, their savoury spread for toast, and Crosse and Blackwell failed for similar reasons, while subsequently Heinz met success with Toast Toppers, an improved product.

Karwad, Reckitts' car polish in a pad, was another failure – a product which the public did not seem to want – while General Foods have tried more than once to launch Jell-O in the UK and again found that there was no demand for it in this country because British housewives find jelly tablets more convenient.

Corfam, Du Pont's synthetic leather for shoes on which Du Pont are said to have lost $80 million before they withdrew it in 1971, was a sad product failure; a long-lasting synthetic product, it could not match leather on position or the cheaper synthetics on price and so fell between two stools.

Possibly the most mysterious failures lie in the tobacco field. A mass of cigarette brands have failed over the years, Kingsway, Olivier, Bristol, Everest, Admiral, Viscount, Sotheby, etc., yet no one really knows why one brand fails and another succeeds. Communication of a suitable image is probably the main factor which makes a cigarette the right or the wrong product for the market and the increasing advertising restrictions in most countries will make it more difficult in the future to launch major products.

Reasons for failure

The examples already mentioned in this chapter show various reasons for failure. The 1966 Nielsen study of 44 failures [2.6] shows that the reasons advanced for failure were as shown in Table 2.1.

Thus the main reason for failure seems to lie in an unacceptable product or pack, while price and lack or trade acceptance were also notable factors. Closer study of eight failures considered by Nielsen shows that they tended to be competitive in price and in marketing support, but few presented a new product idea, none stood out with regard to product quality and in general the distribution levels achieved were low.

The importance of the product itself as the main cause of failure seems inescapable.

When the 200 large US manufacturers were asked by the New Products Institute (see page 20) what were the greatest causes of failure, the replies included such factors as lack of a well thought out marketing programme, lack of pre-testing, lack of market test, impatience, insufficient planning and preparation, lack of understanding of the market, lack of the necessary time and resources to launch successfully.

These are all valid points. They are also very simple factors and I find it surprising that large and sophisticated companies, well-staffed with marketing executives, can have failures for reasons which would often be apparent to the most junior marketing assistant. How can a company risk a large expenditure in the 1970s without knowing what the consumer thinks of the product? How can a company not bother to obtain a feel of the market? How can a company aim for long-term investment in a market known for its fickleness and absence of continuous brand loyalty? How can a company launch a new product these days which is found to be unacceptable by the consumer?

I am convinced that there is one general answer which goes some way to explain this strange phenomenon. The answer is largely *lack of objectivity*.

A company is subject to many pressures. Personal pressures, political pressures, financial pressures, 'action' pressures, etc. The chairman may have a stream of new product ideas and it is difficult to say 'no' every time. The idea develops, from whatever source, and after a certain stage it is difficult

TABLE 2.1

	Main reason, %	All reasons, %
Product/package	53	35
Price/value	20	19
Trade acceptance	18	29
Advertising	9	17
	100	100

to stop it. Everyone becomes enthusiastic, the profit and loss forecasts look good. No wonder that everyone wants the new project to succeed and so it is pushed along and, if by any chance research shows that there are snags, these are minimised and all possible extenuating reasons are invoked for going on. It is unpopular to say 'no'.

Moreover it is not easy for a company to be objective enough to look at itself and see both its strength and its weaknesses. I am sure that there is no such thing as a good or a bad opportunity – it is only good or bad according to the company concerned – and many of the failures suggest that one company can succeed where another fails and vice versa. If this is accepted, it is crucial that a company should examine itself closely to determine what type of market it is most suitable to enter. Yet companies find such introversion difficult and so choose wrong markets. For example, a number of industrial companies in the UK have gone into consumer goods without relating the needs of these markets to their own skills and the results have on the whole been disastrous.

Such lack of objectivity would explain why many of the top companies act as they do. Top management press for action, an opportunity looks good on paper, the company profile is not considered, there is fear of the competition taking the same action. All these factors add up to a compulsive urge to go ahead unless there are strong negatives – and usually the reading is neither black nor white but grey, so interpretation makes it white. The product is launched. A few succeed. Many fail. And then one asks: 'How could such an obvious failure have been launched?'

The picture may seem grossly exaggerated and certainly there are companies where the dangers of lack of objectivity are now recognised and dealt with accordingly. In many large as well as small companies, however, such a situation persists and it is likely that we will see in the years ahead companies with the right organisation and management attitude towards development streaking ahead of their less well-equipped competitors. I have seen signs already of a very small number of companies being considerably more efficient than competitors and so creating more success in the new product area.

3 New product successes

What is a success?

As usual, it is necessary to discuss definitions. What is a new product success?

There is no clear answer, unfortunately, except that it will vary according to the company. In theory, a new product is a success if it meets the company's development criteria. In practice, however, as these criteria so rarely exist, the new product is a success if the company's management just feel that the results are good. This feeling is probably subjective and empirical, yet it can work reasonably well, particularly if the company has launched a number of new products and so has past experience of the way in which they have performed at certain stages in their development.

However a company defines its new product successes, it is clear that what is a success for one company can be a failure for another, depending on the company – its resources, its attitudes, its plans, its criteria. Thus Golden Wonder crisps have eventually proved a great success for Imperial Tobacco, having obtained about half of the large and expanding UK crisp market. Imperial Tobacco, with its considerable resources and the need to diversify from tobacco products, must be gratified at the establishment of such a strong foothold in food. For many other companies, however, the long term investment which proved necessary would have meant that the project was a complete failure.

On the other hand, a new product yielding even £20,000 – £30,000 profit from the first years, which is not capable of much growth from this level, could be a great success for a small company but a complete failure for a large one unable to afford to look after minor brands in case they take the sales force's attention away from the company's major profit earners.

It follows, therefore, that it is impossible to be accurate in calling a new product successful without actually sitting in the particular company's Boardroom. Nevertheless the attempt must be made and I will try to include as many undisputed successes as possible.

Some new product successes

(a) *Wilkinson Sword*

There can be no doubt about the well known success of Wilkinson Sword razor blades. A relatively small family company, Wilkinson Sword made a technical breakthrough in developing a stainless steel blade of consistent quality. Not many would have given much for its chances against the experienced giant, Gillette, yet it proceeded to erode the latter's market share and to become a major force in the world's razor blade markets.

Gilette retaliated, as would be expected, by launching its own stainless steel product with considerable marketing expenditure, but in the ensuing battle Wilkinson Sword has still managed to retain hold of the UK market in volume terms in 1975/6.

It is noteworthy that, although Wilkinson Sword markets a range of products, the success of the razor blade has completely changed the nature of the company which found itself almost overnight as an important force in a large consumer market and quickly adopted the attitudes and organisation which one would expect in a large consumer goods company.

The success of Wilkinson Sword lies clearly in the product itself which had such strong advantages over the other razor blades when it was first launched that it established itself initially despite the lack of marketing support and of a large company organisation.

(b) *Pedigree Petfoods*

The Mars company saw scope in the UK in the 1950s for specialist pet products in view of the enormous cat and dog ownership in this country and the well known British affection for pets which seem to be generally rated higher than children in this country. The idea is extremely simple and had already met with success in the USA. It was superbly executed by Pedigree Petfoods, the Mars subsidiary, which had maintained a dominant share in this market as it developed from cans – still the bulk of the market – to dry and semi-moist products. The total petfood market was worth £160 million in 1975 and Pedigree Petfoods had some 50 per cent of it, but both Quaker and Spillers (who bought R. Wilson's petfood business) have also benefited from the market's buoyancy.

The initial idea was obviously important, but many companies might have had it to be later superseded by tougher competitors. I believe that Pedigree Petfoods' success is mainly due to their singleminded approach to the market; the company was formed, separate from the confectionery side, to market nothing but petfoods, heavy investment was made in modern plant and the products were supported by a strong sales force, professional marketing and large advertising expenditures. Nothing very clever perhaps, just well done. This is unfortunately much rarer than it should be.

(c) *Head and Shoulders Shampoo*

It may be too early in 1976 to hail Head and Shoulders as a success, but I believe that it will be. As already mentioned, shampoo has proved to be a particularly volatile market, but Procter and Gamble had succeeded with Head and Shoulders in the US and finally decided to try it in the UK. With typical Procter and Gamble thoroughness the product was subjected to years of test marketing after all the initial research. Whereas most companies tend to launch many products into the market place and after six months or a year at the most launch nationally – some do not test market at all – Procter and Gamble launch very few indeed, put them into test market for many years, sometimes five or even more, using the test area as a real marketing laboratory and not launching nationally until sure that every possible problem has been ironed out.

 Not many companies can afford such a policy, though some might do well to institute it if they were to calculate the cost of their failures! It has the advantage that, when the product is finally launched, the company puts all its strength behind it and it is not too difficult to obtain distribution because the trade are aware that, if Procter and Gamble launch something, its chances of success are likely to be well above average.

Dandruff is a very common complaint for which there is no lasting solution, but, by incorporating zinc pyrithione into a shampoo, Procter and Gamble seem to have obtained a distinctive product advantage and there are no signs so far that the public have switched off after initial trial. Recently published research [2.6] indicates that as many as 37 per cent of all housewives had bought the product by February/March 1975 and 15 per cent had bought it in the previous month. Moreover the IPC Toiletries survey showed that Head and Shoulders had achieved 6 per cent share of the shampoo market in the first half of 1976.

Extreme thoroughness, prolonged test marketing and product distinctiveness are the main factors which are likely to be responsible for the product's success.

(d) PG Tips Tea Bags

Following the failure of instant tea, the tea market remained stagnant and even declining, being affected by the rapid rise of instant coffee. Then Tetley launched their tea bags, following success in the US, and the convenience of tea bags made them grow rapidly despite their higher price and the conservatism of the UK tea-drinker. By 1973 tea bags were estimated to have reached retail sales of £45 million at retail selling prices representing about 32 per cent of the total tea market and Tetley have forecast that tea bags will account for half the total tea market by 1977-8.

What is particularly interesting is that Tetley are no longer the brand leaders. Just as in the case of fabric softeners and instant mashed potato – new markets where an important company was left to do the pioneering to be later overtaken by new entrants benefiting from good timing – Brooke Bond Oxo watched Tetley build the tea bag market and then launched their own PG Tips Tea Bags in the early 1970s. Within a very short time Brooke Bond achieved excellent distribution and consumer sales – PG Tips was synonymous with tea – and by 1974 brand leadership was claimed.

A most successful launch, PG Tips Tea Bags illustrate the advantages of good timing in a market very close to the company's current operation, so that there was no need to explain to the trade or the consumer the company's interest in tea bags.

(e) Crown Plus Two Paint

In the 1960s ICI had largely developed the DIY domestic paint market with the Dulux brand. Apart from Dulux the market was very fragmented; Berger Jenson & Nicholson had achieved some success with Magicote, a non-drip product, Reed had a large number of small brands, while the rest was accounted for by many small companies. Against this background the chemists at Wall Paper Manufacturers, a Reed Division, developed a good quality non-drip paint which was given the unlikely name of Crown Plus Two. The company decided that paint was an important opportunity area in which it was not performing satisfactorily because of its fragmented products and so launched Crown Plus Two with heavy advertising, launching in a large area of the country without any market or product research until after the launch had been made.

The launch may have been a gamble, but it proved remarkably successful. Crown Plus Two captured an important part of the market and enabled the company to concentrate its paint and wall-paper interests under the Crown name.

Wall Paper Manufacturers own a large number of retail outlets, so the risks of launch were reduced, but only slightly, yet the product was launched simply on the basis of market analysis and a product which chemists were keen on. This may not be an approach recommended by business schools, but the important thing is that it worked – indeed this must be one of the most successful new products of the last ten years! It illustrates the point that new product development and business in general still provide scope for entrepreneurial activity; there is nothing wrong in a hunch, so long as it is right! In this case it was.

(f) Horizon Holidays

After the war a Reuter correspondent, Vladimir Raitz, first saw the cost advantages of packaged air holidays based on large-scale hotel bookings and plane charters. He started by organising a rented holiday camp in Corsica and never looked back. The packaged tour business flourished and Raitz developed his company, Horizon Holidays, as a dependable tour operator always seeking reliable hotels and interesting resorts at prices slightly above the average.

The 'middle class' approach was translated into the literature and the advertising which emphasised its appeal to people who wanted to be left alone when on holiday and did not want to be shepherded. The company prospered and its pricing policy helped to avoid the financial pressures which faced the mass market operators.

Unfortunately Horizon began to cater for the mass market more and more and to seek volume rather than profit. Moreover, as it grew, it did not change its operating methods to cater for its much larger size; financial control problems followed and it was forced to merge into Court line which in turn went into liquidation. Yet the Horizon story is of success as far as new products or services are concerned; it pioneered a new idea, found a specific segment in a growing market and prospered for many years; the failure was largely that of organisation, an aspect which appears so often and which is usually due to changes within the company, directly arising from the success of the new product or service.

(g) Happy House Books

Brooke Bond Oxo's diversification into non-foods [2.7] is still at an early stage, but there are indications of success and there are some interesting points about this venture.

Usually food companies diversify into non-foods by means of acquisition, but in this case Brooke Bond Oxo decided to build from scratch an operation in books and related products. At first sight this had little in common with the company's current food business, but Brooke Bond were keen on the higher margins in non-foods, had knowledge of rack jobbing because of its unique van selling force for tea and coffee, had much expertise in children's tastes through its tea picture cards, owned much artwork and written material used for the cards over the years and even owned its own printing and publishing company.

After an initial analysis of the market which indicated that there was opportunity for paperbacks in grocers, it was decided to do no market or product research; it was much cheaper and more accurate to obtain current paperbacks and to sell in a few shops, learning in the real market place. Stands under the Happy House name were sold in and a great deal was learnt – stock rotation levels, the importance of variety, differences between areas and types of shop, prices, etc. As a result the operation has been expanded nationally and an important number of grocery outlets have Happy House stands.

This launch again is based on an entrepreneurial practical approach which involved learning in the market place at very little risk, a method which, when applicable, has much to recommend it.

(h) Birds Eye Frozen Foods

Following the development of quick-freezing by Clarence Birdseye in the 1920s, Unilever acquired in 1943 the manufacturing and selling rights for the process outside America, but were not able to launch any products till after the war.

Here again there was a clear market gap due to the high proportion of working wives requiring food products without much preparation and willing to pay a little more for the convenience so long as the quality was good.

The quick-freezing process would satisfy these needs in many cases, but it was essential for a large company to pioneer this market for the following reasons:

1 It was necessary to break down the consumer prejudices against convenience products which were very strong after the war, so it was essential to spend large sums on

promotion to 'educate' the consumer.

2 Capital expenditure on plant and equipment was very large, both for manufacturing and for distribution. If prices were to bear any relationship to those of fresh food, it was necessary to seek economies of large scale production, so it was not realistic to consider a small-scale operation. This factor again pointed to large expenditure on promotion to create mass consumer demand.

3 There were considerable problems with the trade, as it was important to persuade them of the potential for frozen food and to help them with the installation of expensive freezing cabinets.

4 Once a certain product range was established, it was necessary to investigate the possibilities of developing a very wide number of quick-frozen products, if the potential of the process was to be realised fully.

Few companies could have had the resources and the experience shown by Unilever in carrying out such a project successfully. The growth of the frozen food marker is well known and in this case the innovator could look at an ever greater prize than usual. The limited space in the freezing cabinet in a retail outlet must lead to above average stock concentration in favour of the market leader and so Birds Eye have made every effort to ensure that their initial market dominance would be maintained. In the event, they have continued to hold the bulk of the market, and have even increased their share in the 1970s, while competitors have found it hard to obtain important shares.

In this case early recognition of the market potential combined with good products and marketing policies which took advantage of Unilever's resources have led to a new product success which has had an important effect on the food industry in Britain and indeed in Europe.

Conclusions

If one considers the successes already described and other products and services which are known to have been successful in recent years, it is striking that much is due to the product itself. This sounds terribly obvious, but the general public often believe that advertising can sell anything, while many marketing experts have felt in the past that they can win by relying on huge financial resources and on superior marketing. This is probably the reason why so many US products have failed in Britain since the war.

The need for a competitive product advantage does not mean that a company needs to find a technological breakthrough, as Wilkinson Sword or Birds Eye did, before launching a new product. Otherwise very few new products would ever be launched. It does mean, however, that good marketing and advertising are not enough or, at any rate, are very expensive in producing results if the product itself does not have a significant consumer benefit. This benefit could be in the product itself, e.g. Wilkinson Sword, in the price, in its packaging, or in the way in which it is distributed to the consumer (Happy House).

For example, the Thomson publication, *Family Circle* owes much of its success to its distribution through supermarkets but even so it would not have been successful if the contents – concentrating on cookery and on recipes – had not been particularly appealing to the housewife.

Similarly, Avon cosmetics have over the last few years obtained a leading share in the UK cosmetic market through their own door-to-door demonstration approach, but again they needed to have high product quality in order to be successful.

Price can obviously be an important factor, depending on the value for money which the consumer believes that he is receiving from a particular product. Thus, Embassy have had a staggering success in the cigarette field by offering to the public not only a cigarette, but also a feeling that they were being thrifty in collecting the coupons. The effect was a function of value which a price advantage could not have possibly achieved by itself. With the current economic problems, price is particularly important, e.g. Libby's C drinks priced below fruit juice have been extremely successful with relatively little promotional backing; the idea of a drink in between fruit juice and squash may not seem very promising at first sight, but the price advantage has proved most important.

At the same time, the value of an above average price in a

 new product launch is too often ignored. If there is an important enough market segment for the higher-priced product, or if the product category is an important purchase for the consumer, so that he or she may actually prefer to pay more for the reassurance of having bought high quality products, then the high price can be a positive benefit. Turtle Wax Car Polish, Horizon Holidays and many products in the fields of cosmetics, cars, gifts and products for babies are good examples. Similarly the partworks, one of the most successful new ventures in publishing, concentrate on specialist subjects at high prices compared with magazines. These high prices may be justified by the small runs but at the same time they must lend greater authority to the published material in the eyes of its specialist readership.

Opportunities for new product successes are greater either in undeveloped markets or in markets where the competition is still production-oriented. Thus Pedigree Petfoods, Tetley and Brooke Bond Oxo found success in a new market, while Crown Plus Two was successful in an established one. G. B. Britton are another good example of a relatively small company which had great success in the traditional shoe market by realising the need for branding. Aided by the new production processes which allowed it to offer a guarantee to the consumer, Britton launched first Tuf for men and then Gluv for women and carved out for themselves a place in a market controlled hitherto by the retail outlets rather than by the brands themselves.

It is widely believed that it is the large companies which succeed in launching new products. For example, in his article in the *Financial Times* [3.1], W. Ransay concluded from his analysis of grocery products that success in new product development is correlated with the size of the company concerned. This may be true of some markets but is certainly not true generally.

Thus only a large company could have developed Birds Eye Frozen Foods. Only a large company could have launched Shield in the very competitive soap market. Only a large company could have launched such a major cigarette brand as Embassy. Only a large company can launch a new car as Ford launched the Cortina, the Capri or the Fiesta.

On the other hand the successes of relatively small companies are remarkable. Wilkinson Sword, Paul Hamlyn's Books for Pleasure and Horizon Holidays are obvious examples. And who would have thought a small company could almost overnight challenge and beat giants in the motor oil market such as Castrol, Shell and Esso? Duckhams did just that.

It is clearly becoming more difficult for the small company to launch new products in highly competitive markets and even if the small company succeeds it is likely to be eventually absorbed in a large group. The resources and the organisation of a large company can, however, also represent a disadvantage, as it is necessarily slow-moving and its executives do not have the entrepreneurial incentives of the small man. I am convinced that in the majority of fields there is still a great opportunity for the small company to launch successful new products.

Finally, two obvious factors have proved again and again to be vitally important: efficiency and good timing. Efficient implementation of initial planning is all too rare and the success of Birds Eye, Pedigree Petfoods and Procter & Gamble owes much to it. In some cases it is linked with very long preparation and evaluation, e.g. Head & Shoulders. In others it is possible to be efficient and yet enter a market extremely quickly, e.g. Happy House, Crown Plus Two. Good timing is also crucial, either to exploit a new market or to enter an established one; the success of PG Tips Tea Bags and Cadbury's Smash Instant Potato shows that, so long as market potential is large enough, there is no need to be first in a market. The PG Tips example also illustrates the importance of a brand as compared with a product, its success owing much to the established PG Tips packet tea. No other company could have been so successful with tea bags as others would have had to build up a brand from scratch. The importance of developing brands rather than products has been well argued by Stephen King recently [3.2].

4 Organisation for development

Importance of right organisation

Although most consumer goods companies are convinced of the importance of innovation, there are great differences in the performance of the companies and these can be largely attributed to two factors which are closely related to each other:

1 Attitude towards development.
2 Organisation for development.

There is a definite relation between the two factors because, although so many company boards talk of innovation, diversification, etc., as vital to their future, not many think this through to ensure that there is an appropriate organisation within the company to evaluate opportunities and to take advantage of the most suitable ones. Yet it is noteworthy that organisation is probably the most important single element in innovation and diversification. Booz, Allen and Hamilton mention that, when they conducted a survey about development problems among US companies which had been relatively successful with new products, the answers were as shown in Table 4.1.

Eight companies out of ten mentioned organisation as a problem and over half the problems concerned organisation – four and a half times as many as those of the next most important factor.

Different types of organisation

Companies adopt different types of organisation and there is no one type which is superior to the others in all cases. A company needs to experiment until it has found the most suitable development organisation for its needs. The most frequent types are as follows:

1 R&D and top management.
2 Brand management.
3 Development committee.
4 Specialist development department.

1 R&D and top management

Historically innovation took place on the initiative of the production side in a company which normally had the technical research and development role. When a technical advance was found, it was communicated to company management and a decision was quickly taken on whether to go ahead or not.

This procedure is much rarer now that we have discovered marketing orientation, but it still takes place in the small company which cannot afford a specialist marketing department and where the day-to-day commercial role is played by top management alone, often by the chief executive. This method has obviously all the virtues of fast communication translating

TABLE 4.1

	Percentage of companies reporting problem	Percentage of problems reported
Organisation	81	55
Control and follow up	35	12
Definition of objectives	26	9
Business analysis	26	9
New ideas and creativity	19	8
Personnel qualifications	14	5
Performance of steps	7	2

 itself into quick and flexible action – one of the main assets of a small company. It cannot, however, provide the thorough planning and evaluation which can be undertaken by other types of organisation within a larger company.

2 *Brand management*

The larger companies have mainly adopted the brand management structure for their marketing needs, whereby marketing executives are assigned one brand or a group of brands for which they are responsible to marketing management. Many of these companies have assigned the marketing responsibility for new products to these brand managers. Either each brand manager is asked to develop new products connected with his range of products or one or more of them have responsibility for some current business as well as for all new products.

Such an arrangement has the important advantage that the person developing new products is well aware of the day-to-day position on the company's current products and so there should be few problems in relating the new product programme to that of the current operation. There should also be no difficulties in deciding whether current or new products demand higher technical development priority.

Nevertheless, I believe that generally it is unsatisfactory to have brand managers responsible for new products. My reasons are as follows:

1 Running brands have always problems demanding urgent attention and it is a brave man who decides to take his mind away from a product currently generating profit (or loss!) in order to think of a hypothetical profit and loss forecast possible seven years hence. Naturally this executive is normally judged on the performance of the current products for which he is responsible, so more often than not the new product side is understandably neglected.

2 If several brand managers look after development projects related to their products, the result is that line extensions may be developed, but no one is looking out for suitable opportunities which may exist outside the company's existing product fields.

3 The qualities of a good brand manager may not necessarily be those of a good new product developer. The latter needs to combine with a strong practical streak analytical aptitudes enabling him to take a cold objective look at the company's future and at the whole range of possible opportunities open to it, in order to select the most suitable ones. This combination is hardly the best one for the executive maximising the day-to-day profit of a product.

The reasons mentioned above and particularly the first one mean that, in practice, I have often found that such an organisation leads to very little development action. I have even come across a well documented case of a company which for various reasons changed its development organisation five times in about five years. After having had brand managers dealing with development, it created a new product development department. It then went back to the old system, after some time recreated the development department, then reverted to brand management and finally settled once more on the specialist department. The correlation between the type of organisation and the level of development activity was most noticeable. To put it bluntly, every time brand management was responsible for development, nothing happened; every time there was a new product development department a great deal of activity was generated.

3 *Development committee*

A development committee often precedes the setting up of a specialist department and sometimes remains even after a department has been established.

Such a committee, normally consisting of the department heads concerned with development, e.g. marketing, sales, finance, R&D, can perform a useful function as a senior Board advising management on development. It also ensures that there is complete understanding of development policy and implementation among the relevant departments.

It is an illusion, however, to believe that such a committee can be a substitute for all the work which an individual needs to do to find and take advantage of an opportunity. The committee can guide and evaluate, but no more.

Many of the larger and more efficient companies now have specialist development departments and it is obvious, in my opinion, that this represents the best type of organisation for development, so long as the size of the company justifies it. Only such a department, removed from the day-to-day worries and responsibilities of the current business, can formulate a detailed development policy for the company and implement it by means of a programme which may include both new product development and acquisitions. Not being restricted by too narrow a view of the business as it currently stands, the department has the scope of thinking in terms of the total field of operation open to the company.

There is, however, a danger that such a department may become classified as 'the backroom egg-heads' of the company, impractical academics who think of wierd technological breakthroughs and produce tons of paper in report form, but are not really attuned to the mundane need for making profit.

It is fatal if such a situation is allowed to develop and so it is absolutely vital that the new product department should act not in isolation but in constant consultation with the other sides of the company, to ensure that there is full agreement with the development programme. After all the technical, marketing and sales departments will need to implement the thinking of the 'developers', so the latter must have the ability of enthusing the others that it will be in their interest to produce and market the new products.

It almost goes without saying that the development department must know fully what happens on current brands' marketing as well as on the R&D side, to ensure the suitability of the development programme. Yet, as an outside consultant, I have introduced more than once the new product development manager to the chemist working on his projects!

On the basis of a survey I carried out among 92 packaged goods companies in April 1975 [4.1] over half – 50 out of 92 – claimed to have a specialist development department. It was disappointing, however, to see at what stage these 50 companies handed over the products or projects:

Before test market	17
After test market	17
After year 1 of national marketing	7
After profitability has been achieved	4
Never	2
Flexible	3

The majority claimed to hand over before or after test market, i.e. before national marketing. This is important and must be wrong as it confirms the new product development executive in a specialist 'egg-head' role which does not include responsibility for implementation and for achieving profit. Such an arrangement means in practice that there is lack of respect for the planner as compared with the doer who takes the project over, the latter often makes arbitrary changes, there are serious continuation problems, both sides blame each other, planners do not obtain experience of implementing and changing their plans in the market place, they lose esteem in the company and the post becomes a transit point to higher things rather than one of the most important and difficult positions within the company.

Because of the various points made above, some disasters have taken place. In one case the marketing department after being handed over a very major project found it difficult to obtain distribution and so decided to increase the sales force. It was later found that, although sales forecasts were met, the project lost money and one of the main reasons was this increase in the sales force and the merchandising expenditure which went with it – these were much higher than had been planned and the difference was not even realised for over two years! In another case a new food product designed for the lower classes had scored very well on all new product tests and in test market. The project was then handed over, the marketing men in charge disliked the product, changed the formulation, did no research, launched nationally and the product was withdrawn after a year. These may be absurd examples but many more can be quoted illustrating the perils of handing over at the wrong time.

By comparison Heinz have shown in the UK what good development organisation can contribute. Charles Lowe [4.2] has described how, after years of little new product activity, he was asked to set up the Heinz development department. He chose only senior Heinz executives, a mixture of technical, financial and commercial men, and they were given considerable profit responsibility. An enormous amount of entrepreneurial activity followed and within a year some products were in the market. Heinz Dairy Custard, Heinz Rice Pudding, Heinz Beefburgers, a range of Dairy Desserts and Toast Toppers – all appear to have proved to be important successful new products. Moreover the senior development executives were still in charge of their projects 4-5 years after national launch, thus ensuring a great sense of commitment as well as of continuity. Finally, as evidence of the importance of this activity, Charles Lowe was recently appointed Managing Director of the UK company.

Everyone in development should study the Heinz approach to organisation with care. Set up a specialist department, put together senior people, ideally from different disciplines, give them maximum power, do not allow any handover at least until profit is being made nationally and possibly never and the chances of success will be immeasurably increased.

New product development and management

The importance of a positive attitude towards development among a company's management has already been touched on. It is important to emphasise this point, however, because a company may have an excellent organisation for development or excellent new product opportunities, yet it is bound to fail in launching new products without the necessary management support.

This may sound obvious, but in fact many opportunities and considerable effort are often wasted in companies. Elaborate projects are worked out – often lasting a number of years – expenditure takes place on technical development and on market research only for management to delay taking a decision on launching in an area or nationally. Such delays need not be due to doubt that the project is a good one. Fear of risk or, to put it bluntly, cowardice is an important element in the delay. At the last minute the board begin to question whether new products are a good thing. It is so much easier and safer to do nothing and hope that profits from existing products are maintained and so the file on the new product launch goes into the proverbial drawer.

It is wrong to criticise such reactions unduly as prudence is essential in development and undue enthusiasm has led to so many failures. What is to be criticised, however, is the fact that so much development work and expenditure have been allowed to take place if the management are not suitably motivated.

It is important, therefore, for the management to have an attitude towards development which is related to the development activity within the company. Either the board should be prepared to back suitable projects which meet defined criteria or it should not allow development activity to take place which will not be acted on.

It follows that in companies where management wants new products it must actively support the development activity through the many trials and tribulations normally associated with each project. Such active support can make a considerable difference to the progress of a new product.

Evidence of management support is shown by the responsibility given to the executives in charge of development. Whatever the organisation, it is important that there should be a direct line to management in order to obtain the necessary support and liaison. This means, therefore, that a senior executive should be in charge of development to have the necessary contact with top management and also to have the authority to push the projects through all the relevant departments in the company. It is not easy to obtain the co-operation of the various departments for a new product when they are normally fully stretched on the important existing products. Therefore, unless an enthusiastic senior executive is there to ensure that the new products are given their due attention, it is too easy for the projects to grind to a halt.

New product development and other departments

Liaison with management and the importance of management support have already been stressed. But this is not

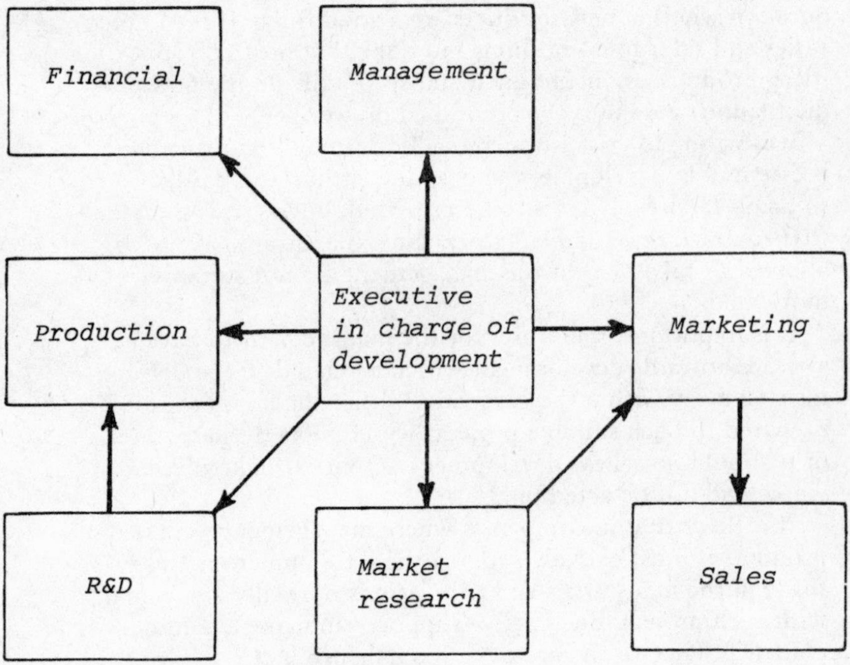

Figure 4.1

enough. It is obvious that development as a function relies on many company departments, but this is not obvious enough to prevent an ivory tower in some companies. Yet the developer, if he is to be successful, needs to become the focal point for his activity within the company.

Whatever the detailed organisation for development, the normal company organisation looks something like that shown in Figure 4.1.

The closest possible relationship must exist with the market research and R&D specialists who will help with the development process as well as with the production, marketing and sales executives who will inherit it at a later stage. Yet, despite this, everyone must be fully involved even at the beginning. I know of instances where the developers worked for years in perfecting a project until they finally unveiled it to the marketing and sales department with the attitude 'Here it is. Is it not marvellous? Take it from here'. It is not surprising that projects are poorly received in such circumstances and that all possible faults are found. It is vital that all the other marketing, sales and production executives should have the chance of contributing at a very early stage. They would find it more difficult to criticise later!

Similarly the closer the contact between development, R&D and market research, the better the results. Ideally R&D should be in the development department rather than being responsible to the production director as usually happens for historical reasons. It is not enough to give R&D a brief and wait for the answer, because in practice development represents a constant series of compromises and formulation changes which can be angled towards consumer requirements, if there is a close team operation between the marketing and the technical specialists.

Problems often arise when it is important to decide on R&D priorities, sometimes between R&D on existing products as against new ones. When I asked packaged goods companies in April 1975 [4.1] who in the company decides in the case of such conflict on priorities the answers were:

25 Managing Director
12 Managing Director with Marketing Director or with R&D or with NPD Manager
29 Marketing Director
6 Marketing Director with R&D or NPD
7 New Product Development Committee
3 NPD Manager
1 NPD Manager with R&D
2 R&D Director/Manager

It is encouraging that in conflicts over priorities either the Managing Director or the Marketing Director is personally involved, indicating that the importance of high involvement in this activity has been recognised.

The attributes of a good development executive

The qualities necessary for the post of a new product development man make him sound a superman. He should have a strong personality capable of generating enthusiasm and of persuading to his point of view both management and other departments. He should be tactful to make others believe when necessary that the project is their idea rather than his. He should be creative, possessing enough imagination to look at the future and foresee opportunities. Yet he must also be analytical, weighing up the risks of each project and the odds of success. Finally, I believe he needs to have a strong pragmatic streak, to ensure that he never puts technique above result. There is a strong temptation to be carried away by the interest of the work into sociology, economics, crystal gazing, etc. Yet the sole purpose of the exercise is to make money through development and no developer should forget this. It follows therefore that a bent for figures is important if financial considerations are to be given their due importance.

In practice, of course, no one person has all the necessary attributes and one needs to compromise as best one can. Once the person has become a developer, it is often found that the post serves as an excellent training ground for it represents possibly one of the most challenging areas in a company and exposes the individual to detailed financial knowledge of the company's operation.

Thus companies may assign to the senior executive in charge of development assistants who, after a spell in development, often move on to other roles within the company. It has been found particularly useful to put such a junior executive in charge of the day-to-day progress of a new product, being responsible to the senior development manager. If the project surmounts the various hurdles and reaches the launching stage when the marketing department or the executives in charge of running brands take over, the junior development executive could well go over to the 'running product' side, to look after the project which he had nursed from the beginning. His knowledge of the project, his experience and usually his enthusiasm often make him into a valuable brand manager and the continuity of the project from development to marketing as a going brand is assured.

As I have already stressed, however, such an arrangement is only worthwhile if companies insist on the unsatisfactory arrangement of early handover. Much preferable is the situation where the development department continues in charge and is shown capable of making money as well as writing reports!

As a consultant, I may be biased, but I do believe that a company should consider the possibility of using an outside consultant, in addition to its organisation, in order to deal with its new product development. Consultants could contribute wide experience in many markets which would probably be far wider than that of the company's executives. Their main contribution, however, would be in providing objective advice, being the only party without any financial interest in the success or failure of a new product.

The problem of preserving objectivity can be particularly acute in connection with new products. Executives within the company are often subjected to severe personal and political pressures, as has already been mentioned, so that the decision whether to proceed with a new idea or not could depend more on who thought of it rather than on its worth.

Moreover new ideas have a way of generating a life of their own within the company. A market study is done, possibly followed by some research. Some technical development takes place. Long-term profit and loss forecasts are prepared showing what are, in writing, splendid figures at the end of perhaps year six or seven. It is not surprising, therefore, that in such circumstances the project is received with constantly greater enthusiasm.

If the project is good, then the enthusiasm is appropriate. If, however, it turns out to look unprofitable for the company, it is in practice extremely difficult for the company to reverse its previous enthusiasm. Every conceivable extenuating argument is sought to explain why the project is better than it looks and so why it should proceed to the next stage. It is tempting to remember the mythical profit figures allocated to the product at the end of the line and so to force the project through to national launch, whatever the indications regarding its failure or success.

Similarly the advertising agency – the only other organisation normally involved in the launch of a new product – will have an important incentive to advise that the project should be progressed as the advertising appropriation spent on the launch would obviously profit the agency. It is improbable that this factor would directly influence an agency with a long term relationship with the company, but it is likely that, almost unconsciously, the agency will be inclined towards a recommendation to proceed with the project.

In the circumstances, when both the company and the agency have an interest in proceeding, it is not surprising that there have been so many disastrous new product launches and often one could have predicted the disaster. The most experienced and sophisticated companies have undergone such disasters and failure in retaining objectivity is the one main reason which I have already advanced for their occurrence.

The role of the consultant is clear, therefore. He can be useful in redressing the balance of attitudes towards the project by counselling caution and asking: 'What are the odds on the project succeeding?' At the same time, a consultant is no substitute for the right company organisation and attitude regarding development. He can only advise, while the responsibility for the development policy and its implementation lie very clearly with the company.

5 Where is the company going?

It is clear that development and diversification in some companies follow a detailed long-term strategy providing guidance on where the company is going. In other companies, on the other hand, there does not seem to be an operating development policy and decisions are taken on an opportunist *ad hoc* basis.

Attitudes against planning

All too often company managements do not think that it is important to ask themselves where the company is going or, if they do ask, they do not strive hard enough to find the answer and to follow the policy thus fashioned.

The general lack of long-range planning is not really surprising for various reasons. The main ones seem to be as follows:

1 *Forecasts are wrong anyway*

Even short-term forecasts are often wrong. Medium and long term ones can be disastrous. The National Plan, for example, prepares with great care in the UK, had to be jettisoned, after only a few months. In the unforeseen market conditions of 1974-6 almost every plan must have been wrong.

In the circumstances, why should a company indulge in planning in order to arrive at misleading conclusions which could prove positively dangerous?

2 *We have done well without planning*

Companies have been most successful till now without formalised planning, often through the entrepreneurial gifts of one man at the top. Changing over to planning procedures is not only expensive but could have a stultifying effect on a company operating flexibly and dynamically according to the needs of the moment.

3 *Planning is expensive*

Long-range planning requires expensive specialists who in turn require considerable budgets to justify their existence. If one bears in mind the inaccuracies of planning and the apparent lack of need for it, costs appear inordinately high.

Arguments such as those mentioned above are strong ones and are often used in justification for the lack of planning. Yet possible the underlying reason is a very simple one – companies live for today only and are afraid of planning which may lead to some sacrifice of the short-term in return for long-term benefits. And this attitude is by no means limited to small companies only. Let me give four examples:

1 Company 'A' was run after the war as a UK subsidiary of a very large US company by a man who was partly remunerated on a commission basis. Being near retirement age, he was clearly not interested in building for the long-term if this meant sacrificing current profits and it was notable that the company lost several opportunities by not backing new products with marketing support which was justified by long-term considerations.

2 Company 'B' is one of the most important international food companies, yet attention is paid to the current year's sales – even ex-factory rather than consumer – without relating the present to the future. Decisions are thus necessarily short-sighted and at times even harmful for the long-term.

3 Company 'C' is again an international company which has had a number of chairmen in recent years. All have made impressive promises to shareholders and long-term policies have had to be abandoned in order to meet the short-term promises.

4 Company 'D' is an international company which sells

what it produces instead of adopting a marketing approach. Its policy is therefore necessarily short-term and it does not recognise the principle of long-term investment which is crucial, of course, to long-range planning.

The need to plan

Despite the arguments already advanced against planning and despite its absence in many companies, this situation cannot continue. In order to survive companies will need to take planning seriously if they are not already doing so.

After all, it was relatively easy for companies to survive in the sellers' markets which existed in most countries after the last war. The balance has since changed and most companies everywhere will agree that they are facing fiercer competition than ever before. Planning must be an important aspect of facing competition. There are important additional factors which make planning so important. The main ones are as follows:

1 *Changes in consumer patterns*

Certain trends can be seen which suggest that the consumer and his habits will change fairly radically within, say, the next twenty years. For example, as a country becomes more prosperous, its expenditure on food falls in relation to total consumer expenditure and there is a trend towards high protein products and against carbohydrates. Thus consumption of products such as bread and potatoes falls, while meat consumption increases correspondingly.

Sociologically there are likely to be changes, tending towards the spread of a middle-class society on the Scandinavian pattern. Age patterns could well be different. For example, in the UK there will be a preponderance of very young and very old people whereas there will be a relative shortage of persons in the intervening age groups. Trends in car ownership, working wives, etc., could all be important. At the same time, the problems of planning have been emphasised by the upheaval in economic trends and in markets since the oil crisis and subsequent inflation in every country since 1974.

2 *Changes in size of companies*

Some forecasts have been made which suggest that in the foreseeable future a small number of companies will dominate consumer markets. For example, H. Dougier [5.1] has suggested that by 1985 the total world market will be more than double its current size and that in some 25 years' time up to 75 per cent of the world's business will be conducted by no more than 200-300 huge corporations, all completely international and organised accordingly. In the UK, the 100 largest manufacturers have advanced from 20 per cent in 1950 to 52 per cent in 1970 and could have 67 per cent by 1980.

However vague such forecasts may be, there has been a clear trend in this direction in many countries and the indications are that in an advanced economy a stage is reached when a few companies achieve domination in consumer goods. If this is accepted a company has a few clear cut alternatives:

1 Go out of business.
2 Aim to be part of a major group, e.g. Cadbury's and Schweppes decided to merge as a result of such a policy.
3 Be small and flexible enough to cater for minority markets which would not be interesting to large groups.
4 Obtain an important franchise which will stand up to competition from a large group, e.g. by controlling its own outlets.

What a company cannot afford to do is to take no decision to cater for such a situation. And planning will obviously be necessary to make a reasonable decision.

3 *Need for new products*

The need to develop new products or diversify has been clearly established if a company wants at least to retain its profits. It is certainly possible to buy companies or launch new products without planning, but the wrong decisions could well be taken unless there are clear goals to be reached. This is terribly obvious but is not done in practice. Yet surely a company needs to decide whether, for example, it is to remain in food or in consumer goods or whether any market is of interest so long as the financial returns are adequate. Only then can one decide whether a development is good or bad according to the agreed policy.

And if there are no clearly defined financial goals, which can only be set up within a proper planning framework, how can any project be judged to be good, bad or indifferent? There is no such thing as a good or a bad project in a vacuum. It is only good or bad in relation to a company's capabilities and aims.

How to plan

The most important thing is for a company's management to decide to plan. This is not enough, however. It must also decide to put the planning into practice. Just to adopt planning procedures because it is 'fashionable' or because the competition are doing it is, of course, a pointless exercise as decisions are then taken which do not take the planning into consideration.

It is particularly important that the management give a lead on these matters or at any rate that they fully accept the implications. There are companies where executives at a lower level are trying desperately to evolve long-term plans for the company without adequate support from the Board. This again is a useless exercise, as the management decisions are taken in complete separation from the planning.

It is vital, however, to understand the limitations as well as the advantages of planning. Some companies have gone overboard on mythical figures for the future and have prepared very detailed 10 or 20 year forecasts. It was always difficult to forecast the long term, but recent events have shown such an approach to be completely unrealistic and this must be true in the future too.

As the world becomes smaller and smaller because of advances in communication, political events must play an increasingly important part in affecting individual markets in every country, as events in the Middle East recently showed.

 And many such events, which cannot be forecast, often have more effect on market trends than local conditions.

The difficulty of long-term forecasting does not obviate the need for planning; it means, however, that a company should take a very different approach according to the time scale:

1 It should adopt a general policy governing the direction in which the company plans to go in the next 5, 10 and 20 years.
2 On the basis of the above it should make outline plans for the next 5 and 10 years, although the time scale must depend, of course, on the development time scale in the areas which the company is operating.
3 Detailed numbers should be put on 1 year and 3 year plans; in consumer goods markets even 5 year plans have proved to be examples of crystal ball gazing rather than dependable forecasts.

Once management accept the need of planning as well as the need to evolve company direction for the long term but detailed planning only for the short term, the method of planning will evolve naturally to fit the particular company's needs [5.2].

One approach useful in laying a framework for planning is as follows:

1 Analysis of company's strengths and weaknesses.
2 Definition of financial criteria.
3 Estimates of future turnover and profits from existing products.
4 Definition of company's field of interest in the long-term.

Such a framework can best be illustrated with a mythical example (see Figure 5.1).

2 *Financial criteria*

1 Return on capital – 12 per cent after tax on Discounted Cash Flow basis.
2 Net profit to average not less than £60,000 per year for each new project in first five years, £150,000 per annum thereafter.

STRENGTHS	WEAKNESSES
Marketing	
High grocery distribution set up to distribute short shelf-life products. Strong company names both with trade and with consumer. Success in marketing mass consumer goods in competitive markets. International franchise and information flow.	Little capacity in sales forces. Strong sales seasonality in summer. High costs of overheads compare badly with competition. No franchise or experience in catering outlets.
Management	
Ability and intention to invest in good opportunities. Determination to plan and implement plans. Efficient organization.	Slow to make decisions. Little recruitment from outside means no experience of markets or techniques not known by company already.
Technical	
Knowledge of food technology. Experience in canning and glass. Little seasonality in production. Some opportunities for increasing capacity on present plant. Favourable attitudes to innovation according to marketing needs.	Lack of freezing and Accelerated Freeze Drying (A.F.D.) facilities. Little technical knowledge of fields outside present product range.

Figure 5.1

3 Break even to occur not later than Year 3 after national launch on a running basis.
4 Cumulative break-even to occur not later than Year 4.
5 Total company profit is to increase at an average of 8 per cent p.a. in real terms for next fifteen years.

The above would be intended not as a strait jacket, but as guidelines. Clearly a company should accept that certain projects will be viable even if some of the criteria are not adhered to, but in these cases the existence of such criteria will ensure that the exceptions made will be conscious rather than unconscious ones. Thus a good reason for proceeding with a project which goes against one or more of the criteria would be if there were compensating advantages, e.g. cumulative break-even is unlikely to occur before Year 6, but the estimated return on capital is 25 per cent after tax.

It is worth pointing out that companies have adopted much tougher investment criteria following the rise in interest rates, cash flow problems and uncertainty about future market trends. Of 92 packaged goods companies questioned in April 1975, 88 agreed that their own investment criteria were tougher than before. This was confirmed when they indicated in which year positive cash flow was now required (Table 5.1).

Nearly all claimed to look for positive cash flow by Year 3 and many sought it in Years 1 and 2. This reflects a more realistic policy of seeking to make money early rather than hoping for large profits eventually on the basis of mythical investment plans.

TABLE 5.1 When positive cash flow is required

Year	Number
1	23
2	31
3	27
4	2
5	5
Variable/NA	4
	92

3 *Estimates of current business*

The life cycle of a product consisting of introduction, growth, maturity, saturation and decline is well known and widely accepted as a theory. Figure 5.2 shows this trend graphically.

Obviously a brand can be revitalised and the life cycle idea is too easily accepted, as already mentioned. In general, however, a business cannot rely on long-term increases in profit by relying on current business alone if it is ambitious to and the pattern shown in Figure 5.3 could result.

4 *The company's field of interest*

This is, of course, crucial. In our mythical company's case it

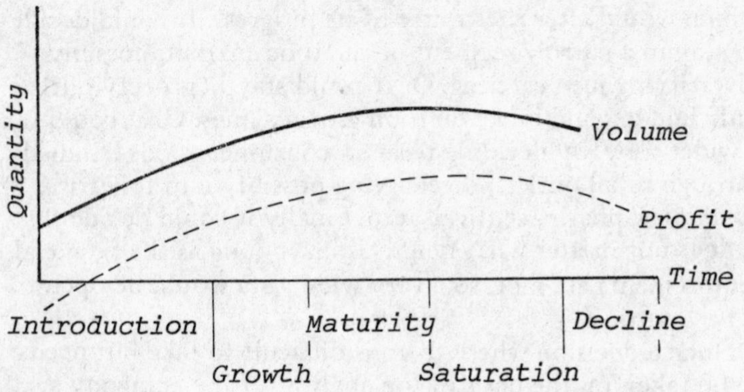

Figure 5.2

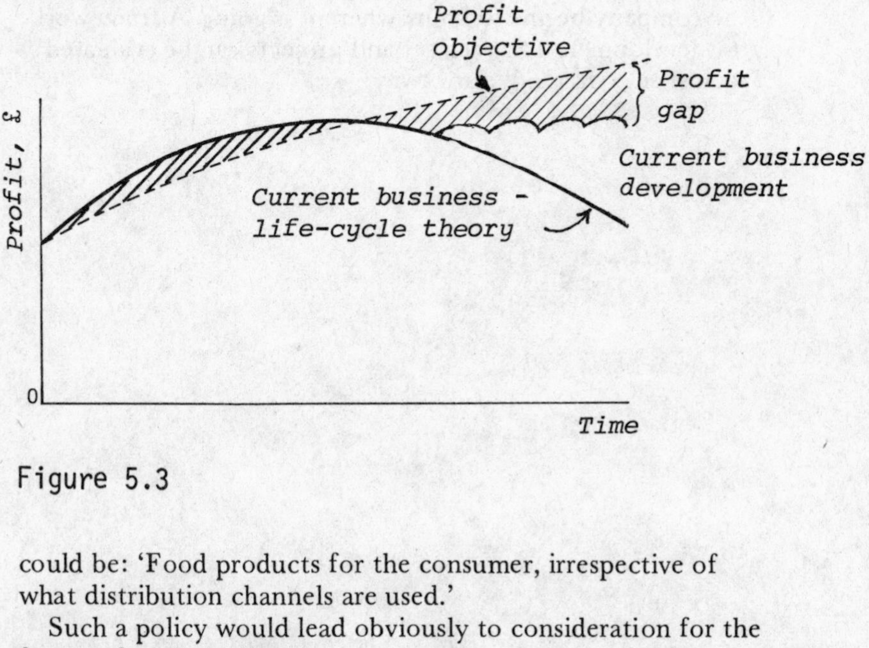

Figure 5.3

could be: 'Food products for the consumer, irrespective of what distribution channels are used.'

Such a policy would lead obviously to consideration for the future of outlets other than current ones, e.g. distribution of food products through garages. A direct approach to the public could also be examined, e.g. van selling on a door-to-door basis. Moreover, the whole food industry would be closely screened to isolate the right opportunities in markets not already covered by the company.

Yet the same company could take vastly different decisions

which would alter the course of its progress. It could decide to stay in a narrow segment of the food market, possibly diversifying into catering. Or it could stay in grocery outlets only and expand into non-food grocery lines. Or it could take a wider view, by deciding to be in consumer goods handled through retail outlets, diversifying possibly into toiletries, cosmetics, pharmaceuticals, etc. Finally it could decide that it does not matter what field it is in, so long as the financial requirements are met, so a very wide vista would be open to it for scrutiny.

Such a decision where to go is difficult to take but needs to be taken on the basis of the analysis of the company's strengths and weaknesses, its financial aims and the 'profit gap'. Once it is made in conjunction with the other criteria, the company begins to know where it is going. A framework for development has been set and projects can be evaluated against set criteria. We are away!

6 Long-range planning

In the first edition of this book there was a chapter extolling the virtues of long-range planning even for fast-moving consumer goods. Since then there has been much long-range planning in the UK. The Long Range Planning Society has flourished; conferences on the subject have produced many eloquent speeches and papers; a number of large companies have established long-range planning departments; technological forecasting has been found as a mystical term describing all kinds of techniques for technical innovation; Delphi models, innovative forecasting, sociological forecasts have been among the fashionable 'in' words.

Yet all this activity has hardly proved itself in practice. The exercise of studying the company's markets for planning purposes may prove useful in itself, but no long-range planning has forecast the sudden changes which have taken place in 1974-5; indeed too many detailed figures, referring to say 20 years in the future, have the danger that they look so accurate that people will believe them! In the United States there have also been serious doubts expressed against too much long-range planning.

Companies should adopt, therefore, a much more flexible and practical approach to long range planning.

1 Company policy A broad company policy should be established governing the direction for company development.

2 Detailed forecasts No detailed forecasts should be produced for a period over three years from the time of the forecast, except in cases of projects specifically requiring such forecasting, e.g. the development of a plane obviously needs a long time scale. Even then allowance must be made for uncertainty beyond three years and very frequent revisions must be made.

In the case of fast-moving consumer goods, if it is required to make a 5 or 10 year plan to justify the project, I suggest that the project should be chopped! It is so easy to put figures down on paper which eventually will lead to a pot of gold, but the pot must arrive very quickly, as most packaged goods companies are now demanding.

3 *Attitude to technology* Let us forget technological forecasting. It is difficult to forecast new technologies and anyway how many companies have made money out of technological innovations? This may seem too extreme an attitude, but it stems from having seen too many consumer goods companies spending millions on fundamental research when they should have concentrated instead on applied research.

Even a company with the necessary resources could decide that the most profitable policy is to be second in a new field rather than first, as George Cyriax has argued [6.1].

Ansoff and Stewart [6.2] believe that a company interested in a field where technological change is important has four basic approaches it can take:

a *Be the first* by pursuing a rigorous policy of technical innovation entailing both high risks and great opportunities.

b *Follow the innovator* by developing again strong R&D resources and an organisation which would allow the company to move extremely fast and copy the innovator, learning from the latter's mistakes.

c *Appeal to specific markets* by adapting the innovator's products to specific market requests.

d *Launch-me-too products*, i.e. launch very similar products to those first marketed by the innovator, aiming to find if possible some kind of advantage in terms of cost or manufacturing method.

Usually, policies *(b)*, *(c)* and *(d)* seem to be the most attractive for a company, although it is difficult to generalise. Much also depends on the time lag in development. Adler [6.3] analysed the time lag in the development of 42 innovative products. According to his findings, the period of time elapsing between the birth of the idea and the subsequent launch amounted to 55 years for television, 30 for zip fasteners, 18 for minute rice, 15 for frozen foods, polaroid cameras, penicillin and Xerox. At the same time Gerber baby foods took only one year and Johnson's liquid shoe polish only 3 years.

Thus the gestation period varies greatly depending on the industry and in many cases is extremely long, though the average length is certain to decrease as technology advances and as technological forecasting serves to focus companies' attention on a small number of technologies.

It is, therefore, important for the company to determine its attitude towards innovation and decide whether it intends to be the innovator, be the second in the market, appeal to specialist markets or launch-me-too products. There is no general answer, as this will depend very much on the company concerned and on the markets in which it is interested.

4 *Relationship between planning and implementation* May planners forgive me, but experience confirms that implementation is more important than the planning. It follows that the most brilliant plans are not worth the paper they are written on unless they are carried out effectively. If they are unlikely to be communicated to the implementers or unless they are likely to be accepted, then the planning is useless. On the other hand really effective implementation of average ideas and plans, although not an ideal combination, can often lead to commercial success. What is not often realised is that successful developments are usually simple, even obvious ideas rather than intellectually exciting ones; it did not require brilliant planning for Mars to go into petfoods or for Brooke Bond Oxo to go into tea bags; what mattered more was the implementation.

7 Isolation of market opportunities

Find the market for the company

When the company's development policy has been established, and if it has been decided to look for new markets, it follows that the next step must be to isolate the most suitable markets for the company, ideally in the context of long-range forecasting.

Although the process of market search sounds simple in theory, in practice it is not. After all there are so many companies in the hunt these days that, if there is an obvious market with great potential for new entrants, one can be assured that dozens of companies are considering it at the same time. Thus a number of companies entered the slimming product field in the early 1960s because it was thought that this market presented considerable growth. The large majority 'retired hurt' when the forecasts were proved to be wrong. Similarly, in consumer appliances most major companies have a dishwasher either ready or near completion, as has already been mentioned. Men's toiletries is another market into which many companies launched products simultaneously with high hopes and generally with poor results. Skillet meals are the latest example of a poor opportunity uncovered by at least 6 companies simultaneously on the basis of US success with disastrous results in the UK.

Moreover it has been proved again and again that there is no such thing as a good or a bad market opportunity. An opportunity is only good or bad for the particular company concerned and what may be excellent for one company could be completely unsuitable even for its nearest competitor and vice versa. The two examples below illustrate this point.

1 A consumer goods company had developed a product which, with some changes in formulation, could enter two

completely different markets. The two alternatives were carefully assessed and financial forecasts were made for both.

It was clear that one opportunity was superior to the other on the basis of the assumptions made. At the same time the better opportunity was riskier than the other, demanding considerably larger marketing expenditures and it involved competition with strong marketing companies.

Such an approach was contrary to the company's experience and attitude, as it had been successful by always trying to be a large fish in a small pond and by avoiding strong competition. It would, therefore, be at a disadvantage in choosing a good but strongly competitive opportunity. Its management would be inexperienced in such a situation. The same would apply in the case of the sales force. The trade would be surprised by such a sudden change in policy. Even the consumer might notice.

It was decided, therefore, to choose the second opportunity which did not require such risks. It needed smaller expenditure and the market was not particularly competitive. It fitted closely with the company's strengths and weaknesses, even though it was recognised to be theoretically the inferior opportunity. And the results so far show the wisdom of the decision.

2 Another consumer goods company believed that its main skill lay in marketing and in meeting tough competition. If the market was really tough it did not matter so long as the opportunity was good enough. The company believed that it could beat most of the competition both in financial resources and in marketing skill.

A market was agreed, therefore, as suitable for diversification which would certainly have been unacceptable to the company in the previous example and would probably have been wrong for most companies without the same attitude and the same resources.

I trust, therefore, that the need to find suitable markets for the individual company has been established. This does not mean that a company must always stay in the same type of market and cannot change its attitudes. It is very much a matter of degree and timing. A company which for 50 years has relied on technological advantages and has not developed much in marketing skills should surely not go into a detergent-type of market without years of gradual and well planned preparation. Companies can change over time, however, Batchelors Foods being a good example of such a long-term transformation, having developed from canned peas, to meals and snacks (Vesta, Savoury Rice) and, most recently, to take-home food outlets.

Screening systems

Once the need is seen to find markets suitable to the company's current profile or to its future characteristics if important changes are planned, it follows that the company's strengths and weaknesses must be examined particularly closely in this context. Such an analysis combined with the development policy criteria should result in the definition of what factors are important in the search for new markets and in the relative importance of each individual factor.

Screening systems have been found useful for this purpose. They incorporate all the relevant factors and it is possible to weight the factors according to their importance.

An example of a screening system which has been used very successfully for some years is shown in Figure 7.1

Such a system, however crude, helps to ensure that all possible factors are taken into consideration and that every market is considered on a comparative basis. Each company should establish its own system and the scores and weighting factors will depend greatly on its characteristics.

If the above screen is applied to say eight markets, the pattern shown in Table 7.1 (page 72) could result. This shows how a screening system can be used. On one sheet of paper eight markets are compared quantitatively on nineteen different factors. The following conclusions can be drawn from the hypothetical figures:

1. Two or three of the markets are clearly more suitable for the company than the others. Even if it would be ridiculous to take small differences in total score too seriously, markets A, E and H are far ahead of the others, while markets D and G are extremely poor.

1. Growth		*Weighting Factor*
a Sterling Sales Trend		3
Declining market	−2	
Static market	−1	
Growth in line with population	0	
Growth faster than population growth	+1	
Growth much faster than population growth	+2	
b Volume Trend		4
Declining unit sales	−2	
Static unit sales	−1	
Growth in line with population	0	
Growth faster than population growth	+1	
Growth much faster than population growth	+2	
c Long-term Prospects		6
Almost certain decline	−2	
Probable decline	−1	
Likely static market	0	
Probable growth	+1	
Almost certain growth	+2	
2. The Market		
a Current Market Size (*R.S.P.*)		3
Under £2m.	−2	
£2m.–10m.	−1	
£11m.–20m.	0	
£20m.–40m.	+1	
£40m.+	+2	
b Buying by Class		1
Strong C2DE bias	−2	
Some C2DE bias	−1	
Strong ABC1 bias	0	
General appeal	+1	
General appeal with some ABC1 bias	+2	
c Age Group Characteristics		2
Concentration among old persons	−2	
Strong bias among older age groups	−1	
Little difference by age	0	
Some bias among young age groups	+1	
Strong bias among young age groups	+2	
d Area Profile		1
Concentration in one or two areas	−2	
Strong regional differences	−1	
National appeal with Northern bias	0	
Uniform appeal nationally	+1	
National appeal with Southern bias	+2	

		Weighting Factor
3. *Stability*		
a Economic Factors		5
Very sensitive to economic conditions	−2	
Fairly sensitive	−1	
Some sensitivity	0	
Should be reasonably stable	+1	
Strong continuous demand	+2	
b Seasonality		3
Sales concentrated in one month of the year	−2	
Strong seasonality in one part of the year	−1	
Two peaks during the year	0	
Some seasonality	+1	
No seasonality	+2	
4. *Marketing Skills*		
a Penetration of Branding		3
Dominated by two or three major brands	−2	
One dominating brand with own brand element	−1	
Fragmentation among many brands	0	
Two or three brands with strong own brand element	+1	
Commodity market moving towards branding	+2	
b Companies in the Market		5
Three or more major marketing companies in market	−2	
Market divided among two major marketing companies	−1	
One major company in market	0	
Market divided among two or three unsophisticated companies	+1	
Market fragmented among a number of unsophisticated companies	+2	
c Marketing/Sales Ratio		3
Very high expenditure	−2	
High expenditure	−1	
Average for consumer goods	0	
Low expenditure	+1	
Very low expenditure	+2	
d Product Differentation		5
Little prospect of product advantage	−2	
Uncertain prospect of product advantage	−1	
Some prospects for slight advantages	0	
Some prospects for important product advantages	+1	
Good prospects for important product advantages	+2	

		Weighting Factor
5. Image		
a Company Image		2
Weakens company image	−2	
Inconsistent with image	−1	
Makes no difference to image	0	
Strengthens image	+1	
Strengthens image very considerably	+2	
b Brand Images		4
Cannot use company brand names	−2	
Unlikely to use brand names	−1	
Can possibly use brand names	0	
Company brand names would be sensible	+1	
Brand names would be positively helpful	+2	
6. Production		
a Technology		5
Very different technology unfamiliar to company required	−2	
Fairly different technology unfamiliar to company	−1	
Different technology but familiar to company	0	
Similar technology	+1	
Similar technology some capacity available	+2	
b Buying Resources		3
Severe buying disadvantage compared with competition	−2	
Some disadvantages	−1	
No difference from competition	0	
Competitive advantages	+1	
Strong buying advantages	+2	
7. Selling and Distribution		
a Sales Force		6
Present sales force completely unsuitable	−2	
Sales force compares badly with competition	−1	
Equal to competition	0	
Some competitive advantages	+1	
Sales force capacity and strong competitive advantage	+2	
b Distribution		5
Completely different outlets from those covered now	−2	
Large extension needed to current distribution	−1	
Some extension needed	0	
Small extension needed	+1	
Present distribution completely suitable	+2	

Figure 7.1

TABLE 7.1

Factor	Maximum score	Market A	B	C	D	E	F	G	H
Sterling sales trend	6	6	0	-6	3	3	0	-3	0
Volume trend	8	4	-4	-8	0	4	0	-4	-4
Long-term prospects	12	0	0	-6	0	12	0	-6	0
Current market size	6	0	6	3	0	0	6	3	-3
Buying by class	2	1	1	1	0	2	1	1	0
Age group characteristics	4	0	0	0	2	2	0	-2	0
Area profile	2	1	1	1	0	2	-1	0	1
Economic factors	10	5	5	0	-5	10	-5	5	0
Seasonality	6	-3	0	0	3	3	6	0	3
Penetration of branding	6	6	0	3	-6	3	0	3	0
Companies in the market	10	10	5	5	-10	5	5	5	5
Marketing/sales ratio	6	3	0	0	-6	3	0	0	3
Product differentiation	10	5	0	5	0	5	0	-5	0
Company image	4	0	2	0	2	-2	2	0	4
Brand images	8	0	0	4	4	0	0	0	8
Technology	10	5	0	-5	-5	-5	0	0	5
Buying resources	6	0	3	0	-3	0	0	3	3
Sales force	12	6	0	6	-6	6	0	0	0
Distribution	10	5	0	5	0	-5	0	0	10
TOTAL	138	54	19	8	-28	48	14	0	35

2 It is rewarding to analyse how the various markets differ. Market A, for example, scores because of rising sales in the past, favourable competitive conditions and suitable sales and distribution facilities. It is notable, however, in its lack of long-term growth prospects unlike Market E. The latter clearly is a fine long-term prospect, but suffers from being different from the company's current production and distribution facilities. Market H, on the other hand, shows no growth prospects and has also had no past growth unlike A. It scores highly by being very suitable for the company's current resources and would benefit from the company's name and brand images.

If the above conclusions are accepted, it follows that it is possible on the basis of the screen to eliminate the completely unsuitable markets and to divide the possibly suitable ones by time, and thus begin to formulate a short- and long-term programme. Thus Market H could present very quick low investment opportunities. Market A would similarly be short-term, while Market E could only be included in a long-term programme.

Once the above conclusions are made, the markets which have been singled out can be analysed in depth in a way which is not possible on a crude screen and doubtless a large proportion will still be eliminated at a later stage.

I hope, however, that the examples have demonstrated the value of the quick sieve at an early stage, however crude. Not only does it ensure that the broadest possible spectrum of opportunities is taken into consideration. It also enables the company to concentrate its attention at a very early stage on a relatively small number of opportunities.

The ability to differentiate between markets and projects at a very early stage is extremely important for the company and it is not easy to achieve this discipline. In practice most companies have a large number of development projects at various stages which they hesitate to kill or postpone, as there is usually some reason why each one has potential promise. Yet because the company hesitates to eliminate the majority of such projects, it is likely to find it difficult to progress any satisfactorily. For example, if the R&D department have, say, forty projects going through the works and if another twenty or thirty are being studied from the market and research angles, the company must suffer from development indigestion. Few if any projects come out at the end of the line and progress is extremely slow because of the diffusion of attention and resources on so many projects.

A quick screen enables the company to abandon or at any rate postpone most of the projects. It may then go on by concentrating on, say, only about a dozen of the most promising ones and the speed with which these can be tackled would be a revelation to most companies. The early isolation of marketing opportunities, even subject to later validation, is a crucial ingredient in a successful development programme.

The use of such numerical screening methods was developed in the 1960s. I have been involved in hundreds and I know that a large number of companies have used them successfully. So long as they are treated as a useful discipline rather than as an accurate forecasting device, they represent one of the more important stages in the development programme.

8 Progress up to national launch

Step-by-step approach

Once the suitable market has been identified and the opportunities have been defined, the development process has, of course, only just begun. One now embarks on the tortuous road leading eventually up to national launch if the project survives all the obstacles in its path.

There are varying attitudes towards the development process starting at this stage. At one end of the scale is the painstaking approach. So many new products fail, so it is vital to measure all the important factors, even if this takes a long time. By the end the product will be so acceptable both to the trade and to the consumer that the painstaking process will be found worthwhile.

At the other end of the scale is the opposite approach. Development can be compared with the sex life of an elephant – at first there is much noise normally in high quarters and then nothing happens for a terribly long time. Because it is so easy to find reasons for more research all the time and because the research normally gives only imperfect answers, this school of thought firmly believes that one must move very fast to produce a product and with the minimum of research launch it in a small test area, say in a town. At this stage the company learns about the attitudes towards the product in the market, and changes in the product and in its marketing can be made and tested in realistic conditions.

As usual the right answer lies somewhere in between the two extremes. A research programme is certainly worthwhile if the risk and the opportunity justify it, but it is impossible to take the risk element out of a development project. In the end, judgement will still be needed on whether to go ahead or not and there will still be important assumptions to make which research has not covered.

It may seem possible to research every important point in a large project, but in practice this is not realistic. In a recent project a great deal of time and money had been spent on formulation of assumptions and on research to validate them. When it was realised, however, that the majority of assumptions had still not been validated, the possibility of doing so was considered and it was found that the research would take another three years, while the cost of it would be astronomical!

At the same time, to move very fast to a town test often means taking important and expensive decisions to reach that stage. A pilot plan may be necessary, the sales force effort, though limited, must affect the sales of the company's other products and a number of town tests at the same time would take up much of the sales force's resources. Similarly there would be expensive use of R&D because very fast progress means that there would be little possibility of cutting the number of projects once they had been selected for development, so they would all go through R&D. Moreover, the marketing budgets even in a town can run to many thousands of pounds if one considers the advertising, trade and consumer promotions, point of sale material and the research necessary to measure the test. Finally, much management time would need to be spent on each project of this nature which could otherwise be allocated to items of more immediate profit to the company.

I believe, therefore, that the best approach is to prepare a programme of progress up to the launch based on a number of steps or hurdles that the project needs to overcome one by one. It is agreed that the path up to the launch is a hazardous one, so the hurdles need to be overcome in turn if the project is to progress. They will vary according to the project. For example, a major and complicated market entry would clearly merit a much more comprehensive programme than a relatively safe range extension which could well justify quick progress to a national launch without preliminary test marketing.

In principle, the initial steps should be inexpensive. They should largely cover areas where assumptions can be made. Then as the project surmounts more and more hurdles and so becomes increasingly viable, there is growing justification in spending money to validate the assumptions through market research and in development of the product through R&D.

Such a step by step approach provides management with a pre-designed number of cut-off points, so that a project needs to progress strictly on its merits if it is to reach the final stages. Yet it need not be slow where speed is important. In practice it has proved itself time and time again as an important discipline in new product development.

The steps

There is no magic list which will apply in every case. Nevertheless a typical list is given below and it should be useful for adaptation to a company's particular needs.

It is assumed that the company has carried out a screening operation, as described in the previous chapter, and that as a result it has narrowed down the list of suitable opportunities to be examined further and to be progressed up to national launch if they continue to look promising. In the circumstances the steps which would follow are:

1 *Preliminary financial evaluation*

The screening process is unlikely to include detailed financial evaluations for every possible opportunity screened. It is important, therefore, to test the financial implications of the short list of selected opportunities in relation to the financial criteria laid down by the company.

At this stage, it is unlikely that much factual information is available, so there is need for the usual assumptions, particularly on such points as cost of goods and cost of plant. Other costs such as distribution, sales force, general overheads, etc. can often be estimated reasonably accurately on the basis of comparisons with the company's other products.

The market trends and shares which the company is likely to obtain can also be extremely difficult to forecast and a careful look at the particular market is necessary, to see what has happened on such occasions in the past. The company's performance in past development products should also be a useful pointer.

At times, the market does not exist at all or is completely undeveloped. In such cases it is necessary to consider the markets which will be affected by the new one. For example, if one were to assess the market for the first hovercraft, there would be, of course, no competition, but one would have to consider instead the market for all other types of transport which would be relevant and forecast the share of this wide market which the hovercraft could achieve at each point in time.

Once the best possible assumptions have been made and the ensuing sales and profits have been calculated, the estimated rate of profit, the investment time and the return on capital employed can be compared with the company criteria.

It may be thought that all this is not worth the paper it is written on at this stage, as so few of the figures are likely to be more than informed guesses. Such criticism is reasonable, but wrong.

In practice it has been found that, however rough, the financial calculations have been invaluable from the earliest stage, so long as the assumptions are clearly recognised and validated as the project progresses. In many cases the early forecasts done by experienced executives can be surprisingly accurate and, in any case, by including them at several stages of a project, the company stresses the importance of the financial aspect – after all nothing else matters. This attitude has been all too rare among the majority of marketing executives, certainly in the UK, but there have been welcome signs of improvement in recent years.

Many of the opportunities will founder at the first financial hurdle, if the figures built into the forecasts are realistic and not over-enthusiastic in a misguided attempt to make the project succeed.

If the project looks financially unsound, it most not go on in the hope that 'something might turn up'. The earlier it is killed the better, in order to save time and money and to channel the company's resources to better projects.

If, however, a project has passed the screen and is financially attractive in terms of the company's criteria, it needs to go on to the next stage. In most cases the opportunity till now has only been defined very broadly, e.g. the refrigerator market or paperback books. The company now needs to establish how it can take advantage of the opportunity which has been uncovered – how it should tackle the refrigerator or paperback market, what reasons will the trade and the consumer have for buying its refrigerators or paperbacks rather than the ones already on the market. There is need for a product concept.

2 *Product concept*

The broad policy for presenting the new product to the public and to the trade will depend, of course, very much on the type of product and on the market. For example, General Foods were able to obtain a large share of the UK instant coffee market simply because they were the second major manufacturer after Nestlé. Their product was very similar and there was nothing in their marketing policy to establish a clear distinction except possibly the slogan 'America's favourite coffee'. Yet when such companies as Lyons and Brooke Bond tried to enter the market later, they failed to secure an important share. The market had no room for more major brands unless possibly they could establish a very distinctive appeal – a most difficult task. Thus General Foods did not need a distinctive product concept at the time of their entry, whereas Lyons and Brooke Bond certainly did later on. Brooke Bond subsequently succeeded, but only when using a distinctive approach based on Brazilian coffee and a refill pack.

It is becoming, however, more and more vital for new products to have distinctive concepts. Those who do not have such a concept either fail or are particularly vulnerable to competition.

Yet it is not always possible to find a concept which is important enough for the consumer. For example, in the late 1950s a glucose drink was launched in the UK which had some technical advantages over Lucozade. These were found, however, not to be important for the consumer and the product failed in test marketing.

Similarly, the great effort by Campbell Soups in the UK has proved extremely expensive not because the condensed idea was not acceptable, but because it was not important enough. The consumer was happy with Heinz and had no reason to eat another similar soup even if it might have some advantages. Paper tissues, on the other hand, had very great advantages in convenience; the public accepted them readily and paid relatively high prices for them.

It is important, therefore, to assess at this stage not only the brand loyalty in the market being examined, but also the level of satisfaction with the current product types and the possibility of product differentiation. Moreover, in a large market, the concept may arise out of market segmentation. For example baby toiletries have achieved some success in the large toiletry market through such a segmentation process. The Mothercare retailing success has been an even better example of good segmentation.

The product concept can arise from real innovation or from lessons learnt from competitors' innovation. Thus Batchelors' Vesta range has been a successful concept for a product first in the field. RHM, on the other hand, were late in the prepackaged cake field with Mr Kipling, but could learn from Lyons' experience to improve their own products. This approach is particularly common with consumer durables which so often have initial teething troubles and so give the opportunity to the second company in the market to produce a superior product.

Whether there is much consumer research on the market being studied or not, again assumptions need normally to be made at this stage on current attitudes towards existing products and the direction towards which a new concept should turn. It is normally worth validating, however, the concepts found, even by means of a few group discussions, which are cheap and often very rewarding.

The assumption to validation process has usually been found far more practical and cost-effective than gap-analysis techniques which tend to be expensive, difficult to understand and often produce useless or obvious results. Such techniques were the rage in the UK in the 1960s but I am glad to say that very few companies still find them worthwhile [8.1].

Moreover it has not been found difficult to find ideas in most markets, so production of a concept and its validation tends to be relatively easy, quick and cheap. Once this is done, it should be possible to see whether a method has been found of exploiting the selected opportunity which gives the consumer and the trade an important reason for buying the product. If there is no such concept, the product should be dropped until such a concept can be found. If there is one, we can go on to the next stage.

3 *Outline marketing plan*

The opportunity has been isolated. It seems financially sound. A strong concept has been found. Now is the time to make the preliminary marketing plan. This should concentrate particularly on the product – its physical attributes, sizes, prices, etc. and on the product concept translated into a marketing and an advertising strategy.

Such a preliminary plan will serve as background to the brief to R&D. It should be reasonably straightforward at this stage to tell R&D that they should aim to develop a product with certain well defined attributes and with detailed costings to achieve. Even if in practice the costings are found to be impossible to achieve, as obviously can happen, a definite costing brief in line with the marketing plan ensures that the final outcome of R&D activity is as close to the needs of the market as possible.

At times it has been found useful to produce advertising material even at this early stage both to test the concept and to serve as a brief to the laboratory. For example, in a market where advertising was a dominant factor, it was decided that it would be impossible to establish the concept and the resulting advertising policy without actually producing the advertisement. This was done in the form of a Press layout and formed an integral part of the outline marketing plan which was passed over to R&D. In another case three different advertising campaigns were prepared illustrating different concepts and product characteristics. In this way the most suitable concept was found and the relevant campaign was part of the brief to R&D.

In any case, in fast moving consumer goods, it is usually useful to visualise the idea in some form or other so that the consumer can understand it. Thus it is common to:

1 Agree a list of concepts to be progressed.

2 Prepare rough packaging or concept boards to explain them.

3 Prepare initial product formulations, especially in food, so that consumers can taste them at the concept research stage and can understand the concept better.

4 Conduct concept research using rough packs, concept boards, initial products.

It may be surprising, but in innumerable such projects I have found the time scale from agreement of the concept list to concept research results to be only 2-3 months and at low cost. Not only does such an approach provide much more insight into consumers' initial reactions but also it is possible to give R&D a much better brief subsequently because it would be based on reactions to colour, taste, texture, general appearance, etc.

4 *Laboratory work*

The stages so far have necessarily been a little theoretical and 'airy fairy'. Now comes the acid test consisting of the translation of all the planning and concept work into practical products.

Companies vary in their attitude towards the relationship between marketing, planning and technical development. Despite the general trend towards marketing orientation, many companies, probably the majority, find it difficult to develop new concepts, particularly in markets new to the company. This means that this factor needs to be taken into account and development outside the experience of the R&D department must be kept to a minimum.

On the other hand, there are marketing companies which believe that in this day and age there should be no important technical problems in developing marketing concepts. If R&D do not have the necessary experience, there must be others with suitable experience whose services can be bought.

Some concepts can in fact present R&D with very difficult technical problems which are found to be either insoluble or need very long development time. The price/performance relationship is of course crucial, because it is no use producing say, the most perfect dishwasher possible for £400 if one wants a fairly high turnover. R&D is and must be a series of compromises between price and performance and it is vital that the technicians should have a detailed understanding of the relative importance of price and performance in each case. Too often unnecessary qualities are built into the product and so make the costings impossible. Perhaps an integral part of the training programme for a R&D technician should be a few weeks on the road, preferably selling new products!

It is also possible that the concept required in the marketing plan is unrealistic but there are others which can be translated into realistic products which seem interesting. Close liaison between R&D and the marketing executives is clearly essential and much flexibility may be necessary; indeed, it is useful to have R&D and marketing executives working together in project teams if possible.

If R&D cannot progress the project satisfactorily, then clearly it dies at this stage. If, however, they develop new product formulations or prototypes, it is important for the relevant product development or marketing executives to check that the R&D work in fact conforms with the original or with the altered brief. If it is found that this is so, it is now possible to proceed to the next stage, i.e. to quantitative product tests with consumers so that the latter are given the chance to show whether the company has been right in assessing their requirements. Product testing follows with all its ramifications.

5 *Consumer testing clearance*

However good the preliminary planning, however good the translation of the planning into a physical product, there must be very good reasons for not finding out the consumer's reaction towards the product. None of us can represent the consumer adequately enough to avoid consumer research at some stage of the development process.

It is easy to say that there is no point if the product is well proven. For example, some years ago a large international company refused to spend a small sum of money to test a new product among the public because, as they said, 'the ingredients and the formulation are identical to everyone else's'. They did not deserve to succeed and they did not. The product was a dismal failure.

Very recently another company had developed a food product over many years which everyone was convinced was much superior to the brand leader. There was much urgency to launch and it really did not seem worthwhile to test the new product. The test did finally take place as a form of insurance and the result was an eye-opener. The consumers declared against the new product almost unanimously on every factor measured. The project was killed and a calamity averted.

The consumer testing is required for three main reasons:

1 To check that the concept, as represented by the product, is acceptable.

2 To check that the product performance meets the required objectives and that there are no important negative answers.

3 To check that the required price is acceptable.

As far as the actual product testing is concerned, this is particularly useful in a negative form. According to current practice the consumer is normally asked for his reaction to the new product in comparison with at least one other already on the market and the products are not labelled in any way. Such comparisons can lead to misleading results if interpreted too literally because in real life the label and everything associated with it can have a great impact on the consumer.

For example, in the case of two food products, 'blind' consumer testing always shows no statistically significant difference between them. In actual sales, however, one of them outsells the other by about 9 : 1 simply because of its much better known name. In another example product A always beats product B about 60:40 only to be outsold by about 7:1. Again a strong name and 'brand image' cause the difference.

It follows, therefore, that a score in relation to the brand leader of say 45:55 cannot be used at all for forecasting the respective market shares if the consumer is not aware of the two products' identity. One can only conclude that the new product is very little, if at all, inferior as a product, though its consumer acceptance in the market place could be very much lower than the well established brand leader. The results can only be used very broadly to answer the questions which only the consumer can answer regarding the new product, however hard the company tries to answer the questions on his or her behalf.

Very often the consumer testing shows criticisms of points which the company has either overlooked or has not considered important. For example, confusing instructions for use can destroy the new product and are nearly always improved following consumer testing. A small blemish in the finish could be the one point which consumers notice when testing furniture. Lack of a parcel rack may bias them against a new car. The first appearance of the product could prejudice them against it even though it provides important consumer benefits.

Certainly the consumer cannot be underestimated. It has been shown time and time again by their actions that consumers notice slight changes in products which even technical experts do not notice. And the consumer may not agree with the expert. I well remember the case of a product which was technically considered superior to all those on the market at the time, yet the consumers voted strongly against the theoretical improvements. The technical director could rant as much as he liked that the public were wrong. It was far easier to change the product than the strongly held views of many millions of people! Price, which is discussed later, has become a crucial factor in new product marketing. Often a new product's virtues over current products are seen and accepted, but this does not mean that consumers are prepared to pay a premium. Price research techniques can be very helpful in this context.

If the consumer verdict is unfavourable and it is not practicable to change the product accordingly to maintain a distinctive advantage over the competition, then again the natural decision is to suspend the project. If the changes are important and can be made, it is usually useful to retest the revised product to ensure that the revisions satisfy the consumer. Eventually the situation is reached when the consumer is satisfied – and this can happen, of course, following the first testing. Once the consumer testing clearance is obtained, the project appears promising indeed and is a crucial step nearer the launch.

Broad plans would already have been made regarding the sales operation for the new product. It is necessary, however, to examine the matter closely at this stage.

Either a new sales operation is needed, which takes considerable time to put in motion, so planning must begin now, or the new product is going to be handled by the existing sales force. If so, the needs of the new product have to be examined with regard both to its own sales and to those of the other lines.

For example, a product can be developed which in theory can easily be handled by the company's current sales force, but in practice the latter cannot give it adequate time, either because they have no capacity for new products or because the new product seems very unimportant in comparison with the current ones.

The questions of sales force capacity and attitude need therefore to be carefully studied, particularly as in this area there is great scope for efficiency. In many product fields, for example, one company uses a sales force of only, say, sixty men, whereas its nearest competitor may have 300. In some markets it may be possible to have a very small sales force, e.g. in chemist goods because of the importance of two or three organisations and of wholesalers all of whom can be contacted even by one man. On the other hand there is also much scope for miscalculations as sales force costs represent an important proportion of the new product's costings.

Sales force capacity to sell new products can be a real problem because priorities are, of course, involved and current products are likely to be given preference. Almost half the companies researched in 1975 claimed sales force capacity to be one of their most important problems in new product development and one of the reasons for the Heinz success has been the way in which the sales force was motivated to give attention to Dairy Custard, Rice Pudding, etc., as well as to soups, baked beans and other current products. Motivation of sales management and of the sales force is a vital task once a product seems likely to be launched.

Let us assume that the broad plans for selling the new product are confirmed at this stage after detailed study and that sales force clearance and co-operation is obtained.

7 *Legal clearance*

Now that the project has reached an advanced stage, it is necessary to check on the various legal implications. The product name or names would probably have been provisionally agreed in the preliminary marketing plan, but the time has come to ensure their registration, if this has not already been done.

In addition, final legal clearance is needed regarding the product formulation, the concept and the packaging and labelling requirements. In many product fields the legal question is crucial, e.g. in the development of medical proprietary products, and a detailed assessment of the relevant legal position may at times be needed much earlier, before the product has been developed.

8 *Product clearance*

The product for the consumer tests may have been produced on a pilot plant or it may have been no more than a prototype, e.g. in the case of a consumer durable. In either case full scale production on a normal plant needs to be carefully considered at this stage. This affects not only costings but also such factors as the product's physical properties and the quality control needed to achieve a consistent standard.

For example, a large UK company recently launched a new consumer durable which found a very high level of consumer acceptance both for the concept and for the product when it was produced in very small batches. Once the product was launched, however, it was proved impossible to maintain adequate quality control within the costings and so the product had to be withdrawn.

It is necessary, therefore, to make a very detailed study of the likely conditions in a full production run including plant costs, capacity, quality control and the costings at different levels of output with a breakdown of fixed and of variable costs.

Experience in this crucial area affects the accuracy of the study. Some companies, even large ones, find it very difficult to estimate the likely cost of goods of a new product and so either the costs of production are in practice far above forecast, leading to disaster, or the estimates are so pessimistic that every project is turned down because of its insufficient profit margins. Other companies, however, have learnt from the launch of numerous new products and from study of past forecasts in relation to the actual figures and are able to produce reasonably accurate estimates. This is obviously an important advantage and possibly many companies could improve by acquiring greater experience in this field. For example, a company would learn a good deal by carrying out an exercise assuming that it had to launch the products which it in fact has been marketing for some time and so could compare its forecasts with the actual figures.

If the product study confirms the broad estimates made previously so that the project still looks promising, one can now move to the last development stages.

9 *Final marketing clearance*

By now it should be possible to take a detailed look at the whole operation. Market research may be necessary to answer a few crucial questions, but otherwise the links in the chain should be coming together.

The financial side can be treated more accurately than before and so the project needs to be re-appraised to see whether it is viable. If it is, final decisions should be taken on the product itself, on its pricing, its packaging, its distribution, its selling and, in general, on its complete marketing plans.

At this point the company needs to decide finally whether to go ahead or not, unless new developments take place later which would affect the decision.

10 *Test marketing clearance*

It is recognised that all the planning in the world cannot replace actual experience in the market place, so it is not surprising that many companies automatically test market new products in an area, to limit their risk.

This is reasonable, so long as it is not automatic. There are occasions when the advantages of quick action and of resul-

ting surprise must outweigh the reasons for test marketing.
Moreover, if the plant for national distribution is the same as for a test area, as is generally the case with consumer durables, there may be little financial reason for test marketing, unless the marketing expenditure is particularly important.

Timing can be crucial in certain product fields, and so an immediate national launch can at times be advisable, so long as the risks are examined closely. For example, Mars who had developed the UK instant mashed potato market with their brand Yeoman found themselves suddenly being challenged in various areas by Cadbury's with Smash. It was probably right for Mars to retaliate by launching nationally a new brand, Dine, before Cadbury's could expand nationally. Recently, there has been more of a trend to national launches: Nestlé launched their dessert, Sweetheart, without test market, while RHM Foods launched a number of brands nationally using only small-scale shop tests beforehand. Risk, speed, security – all are factors to be taken into account.

In general, however, an area test market is an extremely useful last step before national launch because it enables the company to acquire experience of the new product in the market and to have its national plans validated in practice.

Many new products fail in test market. Those which succeed in meeting the objectives laid down are now ready for the last hurdle – national marketing.

11 National marketing

By now, the company should know a great deal about the market in most cases, and the risks of national marketing, though not eliminated, must be very much diminished.

Nevertheless, it is important that the national launch and the plans for future national marketing should be regarded as the last part of the development process. Otherwise is it too easy to make decisions altering the total project and possibly making it unviable.

For example, Company D developed carefully a product up to national launch. At this stage during and after the launch the company increased their marketing expenditure considerably, because of short term pressures, and the project became financially unsound. Under the pressure of events, the company did not take into account the financial plan prepared and agreed during the development programme.

Company E launched a number of products in one market, covering several market sectors, following much preparatory development, including test market. Yet, while it was decided to launch the total range nationally on consideration of the total test results, not enough attention was paid to the individual market sectors. Otherwise some of the products would not have been launched, which later proved a severe burden to the company.

The above examples illustrate the need to consider the national launch and subsequent marketing in the light of the development plans. These often need to be amended, but any changes must be made consciously and their effect on the costings must be calculated carefully. This sounds obvious, but too many companies in the heat of battle take quick decisions without making such considerations and often regret their decisions later.

9 The creative element

Importance of the creative spark

The development process as described in the previous chapter may give the impression of a complicated set of procedures at the end of which the new product emerges and is bound to make millions for the company.

Unfortunately, or perhaps fortunately, life is not like this, otherwise it would be very dull if a reasonable set of procedures could ensure a success. In fact they can only help. There is no substitute, however, even in the age of marketing 'science' and of computers, for the old-fashioned creative spark.

An interesting argument took place in the columns of the *Financial Times* [9.1] between Anthony Harris and me. He argued that the idea was everything and the only successful innovations were those based on a striking new idea. My argument, on the other hand, was that there is no such thing as a good idea in a vacuum. It is only good for a particular company, so it needs to be evolved as part of the planning process.

It is probable in fact that both arguments are right. There is vital need for the creative spark in the new product or service, but I am still convinced that it is useless and even dangerous in isolation. It needs to be related to the company's resources and plans.

The idea in the development process

The place of the concept in the total development process has already been outlined in the previous chapter. Ideally, the creative idea should fit in as shown in Figure 9.1.

Yet too often creative ideas do not wait until the correct

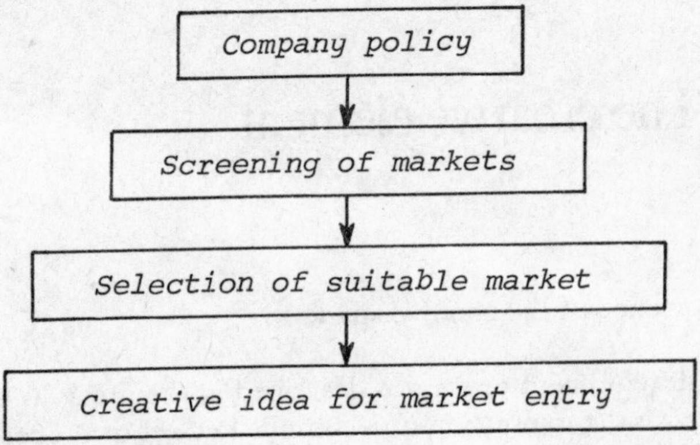

Figure 9.1

stage in the development has been reached. Either the mind is completely barren then or ideas suddenly erupt at any time. Technically based ideas often emerge suddenly, e.g. Crown Plus Two paint.

It would be easy to eliminate all ideas which do not fit in exactly with the correct sequence. This would be stupid, however, as important opportunities would be missed just for the sake of a set of procedures. It is important, therefore, that the company should allow for and encourage ideas at any time.

An alternative evaluation process would then be necessary, starting with the idea. In fact the process would be a reversal of the normal one, as shown in Figure 9.2

If the idea seems interesting, it should be related to a particular market, data on which would be collected. The market

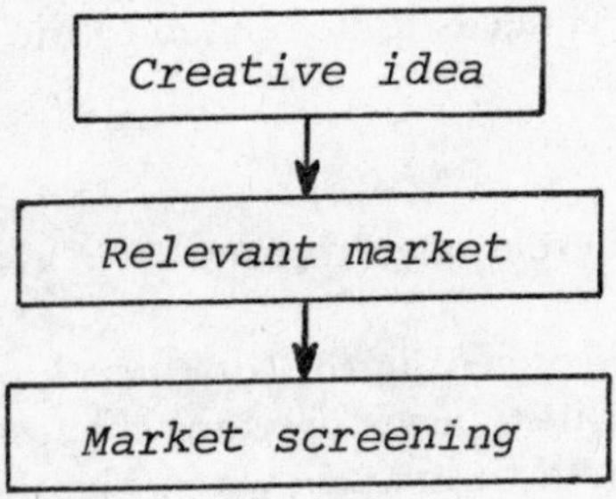

Figure 9.2

would then be screened in comparison with other markets which the company has examined, so that it can be decided whether it is or is not of interest in relation to the others. If it is, one would then proceed to financial evaluation, laboratory work, product testing, etc.

Search for ideas

In practice, there is no one guaranteed source of good ideas and various methods are used to find them. The main ones are the following:

1 Study of company's products abroad

International companies often have a large number of products which they only market in one or two countries. It is not unusual for such a company to have up to, say, 200 products of which not more than 20-30 appear in any one country. What is surprising is that in many cases little or no effort is made to co-ordinate all these products and examine any ideas which could be applied to other countries, although the situation is changing, following the recent growth of international marketing structures.

Examination of all the company's products can often lead to exciting product concepts, particularly if successes in more advanced economies such as the United States or Sweden can be applied to the UK. Normally there is a great advantage if the product already exists and is marketed by the company as there will be expertise available, so long as the differences between countries are realised.

Reckitt & Colman, for example, have met success in the UK with Mr Sheen, the all-purpose furniture polish, after it had done well in Australia. Another Australian product, Fabulon, has done well for Reckitt & Colman in other markets also and seems to have found acceptance in the UK in 1975/6.

2 Study of other products

Unashamed plagiarism of products marketed abroad by other companies can also pay off. The Japanese book is evidence of this in many markets, though more recently they have also led in many technological innovations.

Travel abroad to study latest consumer and trade trends, attendance at international fairs and exhibitions and finally study of foreign literature will serve to provide the necessary information and source of ideas.

So long as the possible need to adapt to UK requirements is recognised, the use of products already existing has great advantages. Such products, by definition, have proved practical on a production line and have found a market, even if in a different country.

3 *Consumer group discussions*

Once the market has been defined, it is possible to hold group discussions among the selected market target to find ideas and discuss them. In practice such discussions are often not particularly fruitful, because the consumer finds it difficult to visualise what does not exist and is too much influenced by the current products in the market. At times, however, they can be useful to obtain a 'feel' of the market and can provide reactions to current products on the basis of which concepts can be created.

4 *Brainstorming sessions*

Brainstorming sessions, if well planned, can be extremely rewarding. They should consist not only of executives concerned with the project but also of some who know nothing about it and so can tackle it with a fresh outlook uninhibited by knowledge.

In practice the session leader should outline the background briefly and possibly stimulate the group with a few initial ideas – even fanciful ones. It is important to let the participants give vent to their imagination and to allow them to put up suggestions, however wild they may be. If every suggestion is met by the reaction: 'it cannot be done', the session soon ends without useful results.

If, however, the right atmosphere and approach are encouraged, such sessions have been found to be absolutely invaluable in practice and to produce a wealth of ideas, which, after careful selection subsequently, can often form the basis for product concepts. If there is a problem in such sessions, it is that they produce too many ideas rather than too few; there is certainly no lack of ideas.

For example, Company G was seeking to take advantage of its very considerable facilities for technological innovation by developing a number of new products representing concepts not existing anywhere in the world. After a market study and screening which isolated the most suitable markets for the company, a series of brainstorming sessions proved to be the most useful method of finding the large number of completely new concepts which was required.

5 *Synectics*

The creative spark may not come from logical thought. Indeed it is better if it does not, as original ideas avoid the problem of developing the same new product as ten other companies at the same point of time – a sadly frequent occurrence.

For this reason lateral thinking methods, particularly synectics, have been found useful in creating new product concepts. The technique is based on the fact that inventions take place when a person has given much thought to a problem without finding a solution until suddenly the solution has appeared through the relationship of the problem to an apparently unrelated situation, e.g. Archimedes found the solution to his problem in the bath, Newton found his under the apple tree, Alastair Pilkington found his watching the lather of washing-up liquid floating on the plates.

Synectics, evolved at Harvard and used a great deal in the US before being used in the UK by a few companies, e.g. Unilever and Dunlop, is an attempt to hold group sessions which the group leader leads to topics apparently unrelated to the problem before finally returning to it and so forcing an analogy. New products such as the De Novo Dunlop tyre have been developed by synectics and after taking part in hundreds of sessions I believe that this is a most useful method of generating ideas, but only in the context of trained groups and group leaders. Moreover I believe that synectics are not always cost-effective and recent experiments combining synectics with traditional brainstorming have proved effective.

6 *Spectrum analysis*

Formal procedures can be used for finding market gaps. A useful one is to examine all the important factors in the market and range the existing products according to these factors. For example, if one were to examine the low-calorie foods market one factor would be their appearance.

Existing products could well be ranged as shown in Figure 9.3. Thus most slimming products do not look like real food.

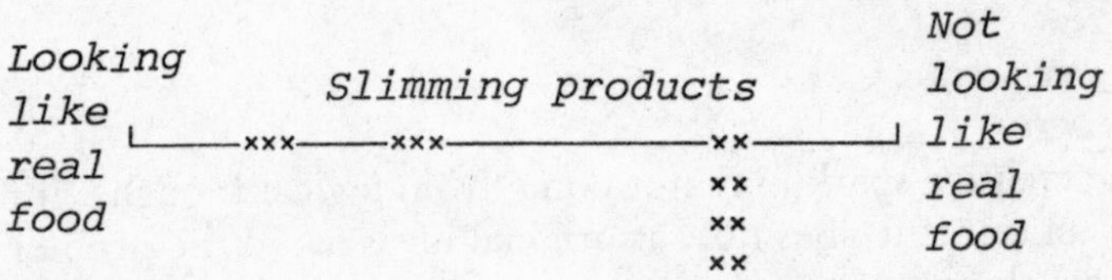

Figure 9.3

Other scales could be fattening/non-fattening, eaten by men/women, masochistic/not masochistic, etc.

When all the relevant factors are examined, the gaps can be put together almost as if on an overlay and gap combinations can lead to interesting concepts.

There are computer programmes catering for this technique, owing to the number of variables which can be used, but as already mentioned, it is not usually cost-effective to spend too much on this kind of activity.

7 *Grid analysis*

Another method of finding product concepts is by segmenting market groups and activities. For examples, if one wants to find a concept for bread, a simple grid could be built as shown in Figure 9.4.

Clearly one can add as many characteristics as one wants

BREAD	*Men*	*Women*	*Children*	*Young*	*Old*	*Middle class*	*Lower class*	*Bachelors*	*Families*	*Weight watchers*	*Non-weight watchers*
For sandwiches											
For toast											
For breakfast											
Flavoured											
Raft for spreads											
Cheap											
Expensive											
Filling											
Not filling											

Figure 9.4

 to on such a grid. What it does provide is a disciplined method for putting down on paper various combinations and again computers can be used to good effect if there is a large number of combinations.

The problem of keeping creative lead

Whether the company is an innovator or an imitator, it faces the serious problem that these days it is relatively simple for competitors to copy its products in a short time.

This is naturally an important factor in development, because if a company spends much time and money in improving on existing products only to be copied by the competition within months, then there is a danger that competitive activity simply cancels out the development effort of every company.

It follows, therefore, that the creative idea should not only incorporate an important product advantage but should also be either exclusive to the company or impossible to copy quickly for various reasons. The problem is particularly acute in fast-moving packaged goods where a company, if it really wants to move, can often introduce a new product in a matter of weeks.

Patents naturally protect the innovator, but in many cases there is nothing patentable in the new product or, if there is a patent, an alternative solution can be quickly found.

It follows, therefore, that one approach in the search for creative ideas is to start by listing all the possible attributes which are exclusive to the company, to see whether they can be applied to the new product. This may seem a reversion to the old fashioned production-orientation, but in fact it is simply use of the company's resources for sound marketing reasons.

If exclusive concepts cannot be found, one may be successful in establishing enough lead time before the competition can copy. There are still technological processes which cannot be copied overnight. The source of raw materials for the products can be contracted for in its entirety, so that the competition would need to create new supply sources. One may still be able to count on specialist plant which may need 2-3 years to be obtained. Study of the competition's management could suggest that they would not move for years. Points such as these play an important role in the selection of the creative idea.

The artificial concept

At times it is possible to build into a product a concept which can be made exclusive to it through advertising even though it is not exclusive as far as physical characteristics are concerned. For example, the words 'good for you' could be applied to almost any product, but having been used for Guinness over many years they have been really appropriated by the product. Thus the goodness concept has been the main reason for the product's success over the years.

Similarly in product fields such as cigarettes or cosmetics, where it is so difficult to find a physical product difference, the personality imparted to the product can in fact become an important product advantage. Thus the approach chosen for Strand, as the cigarette which one can enjoy even when alone, could have been used for almost any cigarette brand, but once it was applied to Strand, it was very difficult to copy. As it happened, the concept misfired but there was no denying its strength even though it was completely artificial.

Likewise, Unicliffe have recently had success in the after-shave market, particularly with Hai Karate. Product differences in after-shaves hardly exist, the distinctiveness coming in the presentation and especially in the advertising. The problem with such a product is that reliance on advertising often leads to margin problems and indeed, Hai Karate is understood to have been much more successful in obtaining volume than profit.

Naturally it is preferable to market the product on the basis of an actual product difference, but if this is impractical the possibility of an artificial concept should not be disregarded from the earliest stages. Even if it can be copied, the first product to use it must have an advantage and what evidence there is suggests that in most consumer goods fields the followers find it hard and relatively expensive to imitate the concept subsequently. It must be borne in mind, however, that in an increasingly consumerist and price conscious world there has been a swing away from artificial concepts towards more factual product/price advantages.

10 Financial evaluation

Financial appraisal in the development process

The importance of financial evaluation has already been mentioned and is self-evident. A development project either will or will not be financially beneficial to the company and this one factor will determine whether it is worthwhile proceeding at each stage of the operation.

This means not only that the company should have standard financial criteria laid down, so that each project can be related to them as well as to other opportunities which may be open to the company at that particular time. It is also vital that systems should be built into the development process enabling the company to assess the financial viability of a project at each stage.

Too often companies make such an evaluation, even very thoroughly, usually taking up much of the accountants' time, but do it once only as it is such a major operation. It is not sufficiently recognised that the figures at the end of twenty or thirty pages of calculations, even if blessed with such impressive names as discounted cash flow, net present value, equivalent mean investment period, etc. are only as good or as bad as the original assumptions on which the figures are based. And these assumptions can change very frequently, sometimes every few days, as the project develops and more is discovered about the market, the production process and the selling operation.

The US study of new products conducted by the New Products Institute Inc. has already been mentioned. When the 200 large US manufacturers of packaged consumer products were asked how the costs which they actually incurred in introducing their new products compared with their estimates, as many as 70 per cent answered that they were higher, 6 per cent said they were lower and 24 per cent that they were on target.

Similarly in the UK costs generally rise as the project develops, quite apart from inflation problems. New plant is not utilised in practice as efficiently as preliminary estimates would indicate, raw material prices may fluctuate and, if the company is in a new market, there is not enough experience in the first few years of how to buy most profitably; the packaging could be charged at the last minute requiring a more expensive material; the planned marketing expenditure levels are found not to be sufficient; more salesmen and greater trade incentives are needed than was forecast in order to reach adequate distribution levels. All these and many other such events are only too common and some provision must be made for their occurrence. Otherwise even a most promising project can easily become a horrible failure if constant track is not kept of the financial changes in the project and of their implications with regard to its viability.

For example, one company recently launched a new product without foreseeing that the sales force needed to devote a considerable amount of time to it if it were to be successful. This was realised in the test market, but the company still went ahead without revising its costings and in the event the product was most disappointing because the company could not afford to give it the necessary attention at the point of sale.

Another company made no attempt to forecast competitors' reaction to its new product and so did not cater for this in the planned marketing expenditure. So when the product was launched and the competition took retaliatory action, the company was forced to support its new product at a rate which made it completely uneconomic and soon led to its withdrawal.

In another case, a company made a very detailed evaluation which showed that a new product was extremely promising and, having decided to go ahead, changed the journey cycle without examining the effect of this on the total project. Already in the test market evidence could be found that the project was unprofitable as it required a far larger sales force than anticipated, but the company only saw that the targeted market share was reached and so launched nationally with very unfortunate results.

Moreover it is possible that genuine mistakes can be made

in financial calculations, if the company relies on one evaluation only. It may be thought that this point cannot be important if a reasonable efficient and sophisticated company is involved in a new product launch, but in fact larger international corporations have suffered disasters simply because someone put in the decimal point in the wrong place or through another such error.

I hope, therefore, that the case is made for very frequent financial appraisals and re-appraisals and for ones readily understood within the company. If a procedure is even 20 per cent less efficient in evaluating a project, it is preferable if it is also simpler, so that:

1 Everyone can understand it.
2 There is less scope for errors.
3 It is quick to use and so can be done frequently.

There are signs that companies have improved their methods of financial evaluation in recent years. Certainly the investment incentives survey conducted in 1965 by the CBI showed that the large companies were more aware than before of accurate techniques and took taxation and investment allowances into consideration to a greater extent than before.

In a company with a number of development projects being progressed at the same time it may be advisable to have an accountant as a member of the development team, to ensure that this aspect of the development process is given its due importance. This would ensure that the accountant is not just the man in the accounts department whose help is suddenly invoked when intricate financial problems arise. He should instead be in continuous touch with the project and have a complete understanding of marketing, the risks and opportunities involved and of the company's resources and needs for the future. He needs in fact to be a well-rounded commercial executive with specialist financial experience. Without this broad experience and constant exposure to the company's general position how can he appreciate the implications of the figures he is asked to calculate?

Many companies will testify to the number of projects which have been wrongly evaluated because the Board accepted the judgement of an accountant who did not really understand the figures on which he had to pronounce. Too often promising projects have been abandoned because long-term trends were not examined and the accountant insisted on an immediate pay-out. Alternatively, some projects have gone ahead to disastrous conclusions because the accountant did not realise the importance of such elements as the competition or trade reaction or consumer preferences.

In this aspect, as in so many others, the attitude of the company management is crucial. It is pointless to have efficient systems and people in order to evaluate a project if the Board, or whoever makes the final decision, cannot use the evaluation. This sounds obvious, but needs saying, because in practice many of the senior executives in the UK are still afraid of figures. How many use and understand even the simpler forms of discounted cash flow in order to decide on important investment decisions? After all, discounted cash flow was described in detail in 1951, twenty-five years ago [10.1], yet some companies still treat it very gingerly as a newfangled gadget.

Yet surely a company's management has few more important functions than to decide on the most profitable methods of investing the company's resources. In this connection, I suggest that a Board of Management should investigate its procedure and organisation for evaluating new products and acquisitions and should ensure that both procedure and organisation are the most efficient and the most suitable in relation to the company's needs. If some self-education is necessary in the process to make full use of these procedures, the company can only benefit.

Evaluation procedures

Companies use a number of different procedures. The main ones can be listed as follows [10.2]:

1 Payback period.
2 Return on capital.
3 Discounted cash flow.

1 Payback period

The company simply calculates the number of years necessary

to recover the cost of the project. Usually depreciation is ignored and it can be calculated both before and after tax.

The system has the virtue of great simplicity and is completely intelligible to everyone in the company. It has some serious drawbacks, however. Even if the implication of investment incentives and of taxation is considered, the method does not take into account the earning life of the project. Thus a project on which the company recovers its investment after five years, which has an expectation of subsequent profits for another ten years, ranks equal to another project which also leads to investment recovery after five years, but which is likely to die shortly afterwards.

Moreover, no allowance is made for the timing of expenditure and income. Clearly the company benefits if expenditure is delayed as long as possible while income comes in as soon as possible, but the payback system does not recognise this factor. If two projects to be assessed had the estimates shown in Table 10.1, they would be ranked equal.

TABLE 10.1

Year	Project A, £'000		Project B, £'000	
	Outflow	Inflow	Outflow	Inflow
1	50	5	20	10
2	10	10	20	20
3	10	55	10	20
Total	70	70	50	50

In both cases it takes three years for cumulative break even to be achieved, but no financial genius is needed to see that Project B seems better than Project A where the company does not recover much of the investment until the third year.

Thus the payback period method can be positively misleading and should not be used on its own although it may have a role to play in conjunction with other methods which compensate for its disadvantages.

Return on capital criteria and methods are probably the most frequently used, but again they present a number of very important disadvantages. There are problems of definition. The profit return normally varies over the years, so should the figures used be an average or the one achieved in the final year? If depreciation is allowed for, it is usually at an artificial rate which is different from the company's investment incentives, while the impact of taxation again is normally not included. Even if the procedure involves accurate estimates of taxation and investment incentives, the two major snags of the payback period method are repeated:

1 The profitable life of the project is not taken into consideration.
2 The evaluation rates £1 in the first year as having the same value as £1 five or more years later.

It must be concluded, therefore, that the return on capital method can again be misleading and would be dangerous to use in isolation.

3 *Discounted cash flow*

Discounted Cash Flow, or DCF as it is commonly called, has already been mentioned as a modern method from which some companies still shy away. It certainly has the disadvantage that it does not represent a familiar process and a considerable amount of calculation is involved.

In practice, however, there are standard computer programmes which can be used to take the drudgery out of the calculations and the system has the great advantage, as the name implies, that allowance is made for the time when the cash inflows and outflows occur by discounting the value of cash the further away it is removed from the present.

There have been a number of books on the subject describing both UK [10.3] and US [10.4] practice. Basically, however, the system combines and treats in the same way both capital expenditure on plant and equipment and operational costs whereas companies usually distinguish between the two and often achieve misleading results. For example, Bodroghy

[10.5] quotes in this connection the interesting example of coal-mining where it is usual to regard the cost of sinking a mine shaft as capital while the cost of tunnels is considered an operational cost. Yet coal can be produced from both or from neither!

Thus capital and operational expenditure differ only in time and should be treated as the same as far as the tax system allows. Naturally the company will need to build into the analysis assumptions covering the following factors:

1 The market size and trends in the total market each year.
2 The market share which will be achieved each year.
3 The translation of the above share into sterling sales and volume at a certain unit price.
4 Average discounts to the trade.
5 Transport costs.
6 Cost of goods on a running basis.
7 Extra cost of sales force and general overheads (it is argued in the chapter on pricing that it is unrealistic to apportion full overheads to new products without taking the marginal profit factors into account).
8 Marketing expenditure, including trade bonuses, trade and consumer promotions, advertising, market research.

As a result the net profit position before tax should become evident on a running basis. Once the company adds on the capital costs of plant and allows for tax on the profits, for stocks and debtors and for investment benefits, the picture emerges of how much money comes in and goes out each year after tax. Of course each item should be in the correct time sequence so that tax payments should be debited to the years when they are actually paid and allowances credited to the years when the company actually receives them.

Finally an assumption needs to be made regarding the residual value of any assets involved at the end of the period evaluated. It is now possible to calculate and discount in comparison both with the company's criteria and with other project competing for the company's limited resources.

Let us assume that there are two new products to be evaluated which, on best judgement, are estimated to have both a life of ten years and to have cash flows over the period as shown in Table 10.2. It can be seen that the capital investment in Product A can be spread over the first two years and

TABLE 10.2

Initial outlay year	Product A, £'000			Project B, £'000		
	Outflow (payments)	Inflow (receipts)	Net cash flow	Outflow (payments)	Inflow (receipts)	Net cash flow
0	100	-	(100)	200	-	(200)
1	150		(150)	100	-	(100)
2	30		(30)	60		(60)
3		55	55	20		(20)
4		80	80		50	50
5		100	100		100	100
6		80	80		120	120
7		50	50		130	130
8		30	30		100	100
9		25	25		50	50
10		20	20		60*	60

*Including residual value of £50,000

that the payout is relatively quick, i.e. the total investment has been recovered in the sixth year. The product begins to fall off then, however, and is almost dead by the eighth year.

Product B, on the other hand, requires the same capital expenditure of £200,000 but before the first year of marketing and its losses initially are heavy, so that the investment is not recovered till the seventh year. It is thought, however, that Product B has better long-term potential than A and so its profits remain at a relatively high level until Year 10 when operating profits will drop sharply but when it is thought that it will still have assets commanding a considerable residual value. How should the company assess the projects on the DCF system?

The simplest DCF method is that which considers the net present value (NPV) and the rate of return or yield of the project. It is usual to regard them as two alternative methods, but in fact they are very closely linked and both lead to the same results. Other DCF methods exist which are more complicated and so probably not as useful in practice.

It must first be agreed that cash today is worth more than cash tomorrow, not for inflationary reasons but in real terms, because investment of available cash will lead to a greater amount in the future or alternatively because availability of cash reduces borrowing and so interest charges.

A public company should consider in calculating the minimum acceptable rate of return what its shareholders could earn on their investment themselves as well as interest costs to the company. Merrett and Sykes have shown that investors in equities earned 6 per cent p.a. compound over the period 1919-1963 in real terms after tax, and estimated that we might expect a level of 7-8 per cent in the next few years.

This obliges the company to try to do at least as well and preferably better for its shareholders, so a minimum return of 9-10 per cent p.a. is by no means unreasonable, depending on the company's policy, the risk of the project, the markets in which the company is operating, etc. Indeed, in times of high interest rates, it could be 12-13 per cent after tax.

If it is assumed that the company adopts the 10 per cent minimum, £110 in a year's time is only worth £100 this year, i.e. £100 next year are discounted by 100/110ths and so are only worth £91 this year. Similarly £100 in two years' time is worth only £83 now.

Discount tables at each rate of interest are readily available and if the company applies the 10 per cent discount to Products A and B the results would be as shown in Table 10.3.

The NPV should be equal to 0 if the project meets the discount criterion and this is almost exactly the case with Product A. Product B, on the other hand, clearly does not make

TABLE 10.3

Year	A Cash flow £'000	B Cash flow £'000	Discount factor	Present value at 10%, £'000 A	B
0	(100)	(200)	1.000	(100)	(200)
1	(150)	(100)	0.909	(136)	(91)
2	(30)	(60)	0.826	(25)	(50)
3	55	(20)	0.751	41	(15)
4	80	50	0.683	55	34
5	100	100	0.621	62	62
6	80	120	0.564	45	68
7	50	130	0.513	26	67
8	30	100	0.467	14	47
9	25	50	0.424	11	21
10	20	60	0.386	8	23
			NET PRESENT VALUE =	1	-34

the 10 per cent discount yield, as its high cash flows in the later years necessarily suffer high discounts, and in fact it can be calculated that it only provides 8 per cent return.

Thus the company has a clear picture of the financial viability of two products in relation to each other and to its set criteria. All the relevant factors are included in the calculation and it can even be argued that the uncertainty of estimating many years ahead is allowed for because of the heavy discount of the later years.

For example, an error of even 50 per cent in Year 10 would make relatively little difference to the projects.

At times, if two projects are compared, one may have a higher DCF yield than the other and yet a lower NPV when both are discounted at the same rates. This can happen when the first one is a smaller or shorter project even though its return is better. In such a case the company, having calculated that both projects meet the desired DCF yield, could well choose the one with the lower rate of return but higher NPV because it is a larger project in actual terms.

I believe that the DCF method which I have tried to describe is simple and considerably ahead of other ways of evaluating the financial standing of a new product or of any investment for that matter. There is no reason why every company should not use this method on a continuous basis.

Consideration of risk

However efficient the DCF method is, it does not, of course, take away the risk in the underlying assumptions. As many as are possible and economic will be checked if the project progresses, but even so a large element of risk will remain.

For example, the cash flows for Products A and B could well have been different if a slightly altered view had been taken and it could happen that Product A could be logically shown to be an absolute disaster instead of returning a 10 per cent DCF yield. Moreover, Product A could be more risky than Product B. What can be done to deal with these problems?

In general it is difficult to do more than employ some arbitrary methods to deal with risk. One is to require a higher return for risky projects. Another is to examine closely the

TABLE 10.4

Project	NPV, £'000				
	-20	-20 - 0	0 - 20	20 - 40	Over 40
X	5%	20%	25%	25%	25%
Y	-	5%	80%	10%	5%

 factors involved in the cash flows and see what variations are possible. If the project has built into it a certain reserve so that if, say, only 75 per cent of the market share target is met the project is still not disastrous, then naturally the company feels safer in proceeding.

It is fairly common to allocate probabilities. For example, Table 10.4 shows the probabilities in percentage terms of achieving certain NPV figures a company may face.

The probabilities would be subjective, but nevertheless have some value if they result from a consensus of opinions held by executives working on the projects. In this particular case the company would need to decide whether to choose the safe Project Y or gamble with Project X with a 50 per cent chance of having an NPV of over £20,000 but equally with a 25 per cent chance of a negative NPV.

An interesting approach to risk in relation to the rate of return was described in the *Harvard Business Review* [10.6] by Plotkin and Conrad who tried to see if there was in US industry a correlation between the two factors, defining risk as the uncertainty in anticipating a certain outcome.

Risk was quantified by the dispersion in the return on capital of individual companies in an industry, a high dispersion signifying a high degree of risk and vice versa.

Study of 783 companies operating in 59 major Standard Industrial Classification (SIC) fields of business over the period 1950-1965 showed in fact that a very close correlation between the dispersion factors and the return on capital does exist. Thus the highest variance in return on capital in the industries studied was in radio and TV broadcasting which also gave the highest return, whereas aluminium producers had the lowest variance and were very close to the lowest rate of return.

This study is very encouraging as the concept is simple and practical. It seems worth while studying in a similar way the variance and the return on capital in various UK markets, so that the company would have a yardstick for selecting a certain rate of return corresponding with the amount of risk in a particular market.

11 The name

What is there in a name?

When the time comes to discuss the name of a new product, even a well-organised and sophisticated company can go through the most extraordinary contortions to try and find one. Lists are compiled, subjective judgements are made, the chairman's and directors' wives are involved and finally, after a large amount of senior executive time has been spent on the matter, a name is finalised.

Yet how important is a brand name? Would Omo have fared better or worse if it has been named differently? Would Kenwood consumer durables have had a different fate if the company's founder had not been called Mr Ken Wood?

Although I have seen no factual evidence on this matter, it does not seem likely that the brand name plays an important part in the new product's success or failure. So many successful products have names which go against all the modern rules of name selection – they are difficult to pronounce, or can be confused with other names or have negative connotations – and yet continue to sell and to flourish.

For example, one would think that the confusion between Sunfresh and Suncrush must be against at least one of them and yet both are important brands of fruit squash. Volkswagen again do not seem to have suffered from what is a difficult name to roll off English tongues, while fibres such as Terylene, Crimplene and Enkalon have become known despite their names.

The brand name seems, therefore, relatively unimportant and certainly deserves less attention than is commonly given to it. So long as it does not arouse any strong negative reactions among its potential consumers, a name which is distinctive and easy to pronounce will be adequate for most products. What is far more important is the company's total naming policy in relation to both its existing and its new products.

The only exception is when the company tries to concentrate on the name, in the absence of any other physical or conceptual advantages over the competition, as the main selling point for the new product. For example, when Carreras launched Guards, the name seemed to represent the promotional platform and the company were able to exploit to the full the links with the Guards. Similarly, some new products have been particularly successful because of association with specific characters, e.g. the Batman Car in the toy market, or Pooh Bear Hunny Pudding in General Foods new range.

Clearly, in such cases as mentioned above, the name is the most important or one of the most important ingredients of the new product and so great care needs to be taken to ensure that it is suitable for the product, for the company launching it and for the market. These examples are very rare, however, occurring mainly in industries where it is impossible to achieve any product differentiation. If it is possible to do so, it is certainly advisable to aim for such differentiation rather than depend on the name alone – a tenuous reason for a new market entry.

Company, range or brand names?

There are widely diverging views regarding the importance of the company name in relation to a range name and a brand name and often a company adopts different policies with different products.

A clear example of two opposite policies comes from the confectionery field if one compares Mars and Cadbury's. Mars obviously believe in individual branding and, apart from the Mars bar, its products have individual identities dissociated from the Mars name. Cadbury's, on the other hand, have used their name as an umbrella for a wide range of chocolate and sugar confectionery products and have continued this policy, though not always to the same extent, when diversifying into other food fields.

Another approach is provided by a company such as CPC (UK) which uses the Brown & Polson name for some products, e.g. cornflour and blancmange, but uses the Knorr name for a range of its products and a brand name such as Mazola for an individual product.

The Mars approach has a number of advantages:

1 Each brand is given a clear identity with concentration

of the promotional effort on the brand rather than on the company name.

2 If a brand does not succeed, or for some reason attracts an unfavourable reputation with the consumer, the other company brands do not suffer.

3 The company is able to market a number of directly competitive brands in the same market. The activities of Procter and Gamble and of Unilever in the detergent market are a good example of this.

The above advantages have serious corresponding disadvantages. The promotional concentration on each brand means that considerable expenditure is needed for each brand separately as there is no benefit from other consumer expenditure carried out by the company. There are, therefore, very few companies which can afford to carry out this policy.

Moreover, just as no other company brand can suffer if a particular brand fails, so success does not benefit any other brand either. It is a hazardous and lengthy business to develop a successful brand and to build it up to high sales and profit levels. It may seem unfortunate that, if this is achieved, the operation needs to be repeated for another brand from the same starting point without benefit from the previous success.

There are, therefore, definite advantages in marketing brands under the company name:

1 Every penny spent on promotion is used to increase the company franchise and so that of all its brands.

2 The cost is certainly lower than if the company uses the Mars approach.

3 There is a secondary public relations advantage. The public become conscious of the company's activities and so the company can benefit in many circumstances, e.g. if it has a public share flotation.

4 If the company obtains a favourable image, this must help any diversification into unfamiliar fields. For example, in its recent diversification efforts into various food fields, Cadbury's must have found their name to be one of their most important assets. Thus, one of the reasons why Cadbury's succeeded in the instant mashed potato market was the reassurance provided by the name in the case of a dry product, which still reminded some housewives of the wartime Pom.

If Procter and Gamble, on the other hand, were to go into a new field, say into cooking oil which they market in the United States, from the consumer point of view they might as well be a new unknown company launching in Britain. Likewise when Mars launched Remus toy kits in 1976, the range took no advantage of the Mars consumer franchise.

The use of range names is a useful compromise between the opposite Mars and Cadbury approaches. It enables a company to invest in a range which will benefit a group of products rather than one brand only and so must be cheaper than the individual brand approach. It also gives the company more flexibility than it would have using the company name only, because it is easier to market product ranges which would not be suitable for the company name.

In general the large majority of companies would be well advised to market products under either their company name or range names. They cannot afford to do otherwise and to waste what is often their most important asset – a name or number of names known and respected by the consumer. It is noteworthy that Jeyes announced that, following market research, they had decided to switch their policy of marketing individual brands such as Ibcol disinfectant and Sanilav lavatory cleaner to make use of the Jeyes name as a promotional umbrella. Even Procter & Gamble have begun to show the company name in their promotion, though at a low level.

If this argument is accepted, it follows that the company needs to know what its name or names mean to the consumer and whether they can be used for new products. Unless the company has such resources that it can disregard this point, its development and diversification policies will be seriously affected by the consumer relation to its names.

Moreover, once a company has such a name in its keeping, it is very valuable – often its most valuable asset – and great care needs to be taken to ensure that the name continues to be projected in front of the consumer and of the trade and that it is not devalued in any way. This means, of course, that the marketing policy on the company's existing products needs to take into account not only these products' needs but also the possibility of future new products being launched under the same name.

For example, Company Y had developed a range of successful consumer products after the war and by the late 1950s the brand name under which they were all marketed had achieved a very good image, implying high quality products justifying an above average price. In the last seven or eight years, however, the company decided to pursue a policy of aggressive price cutting and much of its marketing expenditure has been spent either on special bonuses to the trade or on consumer price-off promotions. In the short term, the results have been reasonable, but the implications for the long term are disastrous. The high quality name has now become associated with a bargain basement type of product which is never at a constant price, being always price cut. The results achieved during the 1950s in acquiring the high quality image have been dissipated and the company now finds it very difficult to use the brand name for new products. Either a new name needs to be found, with the resulting increase in promotional expenditure, or the policy on the existing brands needs to be reversed again to recover the lost image – a lengthy and again expensive process. On the other hand, Tate & Lyle have long had an unexploited asset in its brand names and recent use of Lyle in Lyle's Golden Spread and Lyle's Treacle has confirmed this handsomely.

Name and the consumer

Consumer research can be conducted to find out what the company names mean to the consumer. This is straightforward when related to the company's existing products, but it is not easy to establish what new products the names would be suitable for.

One solution is to face the consumer with an actual list of markets in which the company is interested and the results are often clear cut. For example, Raleigh, who have been recently trying to diversify from their bicycle business, would find it important to know whether their franchise is in products for boys, in wheeled products, in mechanical products, etc. Thus a food company such as Heinz, marketing mainly mass market products and a great exponent of the company name policy (see page 46), may find it difficult to market very up-market products.

It is, of course, possible to change the meaning of a name. It would be conceivable for Heinz to market eventually even non-food lines. It is clear, however, that the further the company moves from the present 'image' the more difficult the problem and the greater the expenditure needed to go into the new market.

Name and the trade

From the trade's point of view a naming policy is much less important as the trade are well aware, of course, of manufacturers' activities in their markets, whatever the name given to each product.

It is well worth while, however, to explain carefully to the trade the company's naming policy, so that they can understand it and can also reflect it in their in-store siting and merchandising activities.

Name selection

The arguments already mentioned show that the important factor is the company's naming policy. Once this is established, if brand names are needed, as is usual, their selection should be a quick and simple process. Synectics have been found useful in producing many names quickly. Lists should be screened from the point of view of both registrability as well as suitability for the product and a short list should be included in consumer testing to cater for strong negative reactions. If it is shown that there are no negative reactions to a particular name, or number of names, the decision should be made quickly, so that attention can be given to some of the more real problems connected with the new product.

12 The price

Current practice

It is not even true to say now that every new product must have a price. Following the abolition of Resale Price Maintenance on most consumer products, the manufacturer can just decide on trade terms and let the retailer fix the price. Nevertheless, even if not governed by RPM, the majority of companies either fix the recommended price or, even if they do not, they must have a certain average retail price in mind when settling on trade terms. How is the retail price reached?

In practice not enough thought has been given to the retail price though this is now changing and in the difficult economic times companies have been concentrating much more on this area. Two factors are considered as the most important:

1 The net profit before tax after the costs of production, distribution and marketing have been accounted for together with an allocation of general and sales force overheads.

2 The retail selling price of products already in the market which are regarded as the nearest competitors to the new product.

If the competitive price can be equalled or bettered and there is an adequate profit margin, the company goes ahead and that is it. The price problem is solved.

Such an approach has the great virtue of simplicity and can work reasonably well. Whatever the economist or statistician has to say about pricing in terms of sophisticated pricing models, the marketer has neither the methods nor the time nor the money to measure intricate demand curves or other consumer response curves [12.1].

At the same time to decide on the basis of what the costs happen to be and what other products cost without reference to any other factor ignores the importance of an important force in this decision – the ultimate consumer. How much is he or she ultimately prepared to pay? This is the point which, as so many companies have at last begun to realise, is absolutely crucial.

The most modern procedure is to try to set the retail price which the market will bear, i.e. which enough consumers will be willing to pay to generate the most profitable short- and long-term sales volume for the product.

The long-term element needs to be introduced because, to quote Alfred Oxenfeldt [12.2], the question is not what is the most that the company can receive for the item quickly. Repeat purchasing as related to price is obviously important in most cases and so is possible reaction by other companies. For example, a high price accepted by the public may not be the most acceptable solution if it allows the entry into the market of a competitor at a lower price. Thus in this case the initial high price, however acceptable, could lead to a later decline in sales volume and in profits whereas a less greedy price at the outset may have served to block entry by new companies into the market.

A good example of a profitable policy based on low retail prices is provided by a small and private UK company which has dominated a particular food market in the UK for many years. The market grew substantially and attracted the attention of several large companies because of its potential and because they felt that the competition was relatively weak. Yet at least three companies found, after detailed market study and research, that the allegedly unsophisticated company was producing an excellent product in consumer terms and had kept its prices so low that they could do no more than offer product parity at much higher prices. The small company will probably never know how this low price policy – if it is a deliberate policy – has enabled it to keep the lion's share of a growing market and has prevented any effective competition.

At the same time, there are many examples of companies which have suffered by pitching their prices low and so found that in a competitive situation they were not able to raise them and had no room for an adequate margin to cover both marketing expenditure and profit. When there are price regulations limiting later price increases, too low a profit initially is dangerous.

The pricing policy needs certainly to be adapted to particular markets as there are considerable variations between markets in consumer price sensitivity. André Gabor, Clive Granger and Tony Sowter of Nottingham University [12.3] have done particularly useful work in comparing a number of markets in this area, but in general companies do not have enough reliable information on the degree of elasticity or inelasticity in consumer prices on the basis of which they can make procing decisions. The importance of price and companies' lack of knowledge have both increased considerably following the inflation of 1974-6.

Even so it is known that there are certain markets which can not only bear premium pricing, but may even favour it. For example, it is almost a marketing cliché that there have been cases when sales of certain cosmetic products have actually gone up following price increases. Consumer durables, e.g. cars, can also come in this category as the consumer buys not the car but the image.

Even in simple food markets, some brands have been very successful though priced considerably above the competition. The branding policy has been able to justify the extra price. In this context one needs to note particularly the role of advertising in the promotion of a selling concept which may not be based on any product advantage and yet is striking enough to warrant the high price. In fact the advertising and the resulting brand image become almost a product ingredient.

On the other hand, the consumer and specifically the housewife is much more price conscious than one would expect [12.4].

Since decimalisation and raging inflation, however, price consciousness has become low, as many surveys have shown, but interest in price has become intense. In grocery products the importance of self-service outlets has meant that the housewife can easily compare prices in the shop even if she is confused about them. Unit prices are becoming increasingly important and there is a suggestion that in many markets there will be a trend to small sizes rather than bulk packs.

I believe that many new products have failed because they were too highly priced; for example Colmans produced a delicious squash with honey which proved too expensive in a very price-conscious commodity market. Likewise many aerosol products have failed because the aerosol packaging is expensive and cannot justify the extra cost compared with more traditional cheaper containers, unless there are special reasons to have an aerosol rather than say a squeeze pack, as indeed is the case with hair-sprays. Equally the many food convenience products, e.g. ready meals, have tended to be expensive; indeed food manufacturers have for the last few years made numerous attempts to introduce new products representing some advantage over current ones but invariably at a higher price; not enough effort has gone into offering lower priced products to the public. For example, Viota succeeded with the Economix range of cake mixes priced lower by abandoning the outer carton, Crosse and Blackwell have done well with Chef soups at lower unit prices than other packet soups, while Heinz Creamed Rice was launched as a superior product but at the same price as other products, as Heinz did not believe they could obtain a price premium. Here is a lesson for others to follow.

There are obvious pricing problems if a company enters an existing market, but even if it can be wrong to try to match the competition their price serves as a useful reference. Yet, if these markets present pricing problems, what about the market which does not exist at all, so that there is no reference point?

In practice, the problem, if it is not to be treated completely subjectively, is extremely complex. At times a reference point can still be found by relating the entirely new product to the cost of products it may supersede or may be comparable to in the public eye. Thus the price of a hovercraft, though it is completely new, will need to be at least related to that of other forms of transport. A complete pie-kit product, e.g. Unilever's Promise, needs to be related to the cost on the one hand of buying ready-made pies and on the other to that of home baking. The first launderette should have had some reference to the cost of alternative methods of washing. It is in fact extremely rare that an innovation occurs which does not replace some current activities and so cannot be related to them in price.

Yet, even if reference points are found, how can one find out how much the market will bear? How much is a certain competitive advantage or a certain level of convenience worth in terms of price? These are questions which certainly need to be tackled.

Pricing research

Despite the advances made in market research in recent years, it must be admitted that there is still some way to go before one can be satisfied with the market research in the field of pricing.

Ideally answers to such questions as 'Will you buy the product at 10p?' or 'How much more would you be willing to pay for this product than for what you normally buy?' should give an indication of the price for a new product and of the likely volume of sales at that price.

In practice, however, the problem lies in reconciling answers to such questions as the above with actual intention to purchase and with real purchasing rates. The consumer answers tend to be much too helpful as the consumer believes that the company wants to hear that he or she will buy from it in the future and the exaggeration factor can easily vary considerably according to the characteristics of each market.

A very common type of problem follows. If, say, one requires 5 per cent of all housewives to be regular buyers of the new product in order to meet the financial criteria set for the project and 15 per cent of a housewife sample say that they would be happy to buy the product regularly at the required price, is the research result good, bad or indifferent?

In-store tests or selling the new product at two prices on a mini-van are methods which have been used, but they are not completely satisfactory either; store tests require an impossible amount of control over many variables in the store, as competitive activity even in an indirectly related field can throw the results completely. Moreover such tests imply that a reasonable amount of finished packaged product is available, whereas the pricing information is usually so crucial that it is required at an earlier stage, as negative results may mean that the project should not be progressed.

Since 1971 I have been closely involved with André Gabor, Clive Granger and Tony Sowter in using their pricing techniques to help answer the question for a new product – 'What will the market bear?'

The methods evolved have been described at a number of conferences and in many papers [12.5-12.8] and, although they require artificial research situation, the results have been found extremely useful in many cases.

The method, briefly, is based on interviews with target consumers usually in hall situations, where respondents are shown a representation of the new product, usually aided by a concept board, a dummy pack or even a video-tape TV film and are asked buy-response questions, i.e. whether they would or would not buy it at each of a number of prices in randomised order. The results can be shown visually as in Figure 12.1. Such a buy-response curve means little in isolation, but, if it is possible to compare it with many other such curves, useful conclusions can be drawn regarding the percentage of respondents saying that they will buy at each price and the steepness of the slope as the price rises. Moreover, buy-response questions are also usually asked for any variables in the new product, e.g. for different forms of packaging or presentation, as well as for competitors already on the market. In this way differentials can be seen from the current products and between any alternative forms for the new product. Many other questions – attitude questions, choices questions between products shown side by side in different price situations,

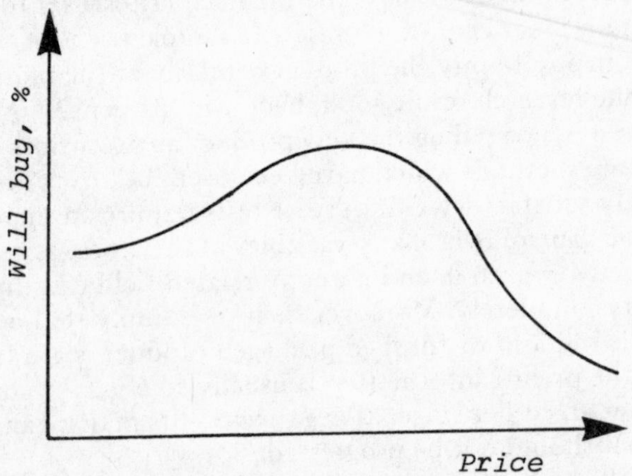

Figure 12.1 New product buy response

etc. – help to build up a picture of price sensitivity which, though not perfect, cannot be obtained in any other way, in my opinion. Even if the absolute price reactions are of limited value in an inflationary situation, the differentials hold good and are useful whatever the inflation rate.

Moreover it has sometimes been important to repeat the same kind of questions after consumers have been given the new product to try and use at home. For example, a cold remedy was shown to cold sufferers who liked it but said that they would not pay the premium price which the company required. The cold sufferers were then given the product to use at home and in general they were pleased with it and recognised its advantages, but the price answers again confirmed that they would not pay more for it, so the project was dropped. Soon after another company launched the identical product at a high price and the poor consumer sales which they achieved amply proved that the pricing research results were correct.

In another case a new type of product was being considered at a very low unit price; pricing research showed that it could not be launched at 3½p but 3p was possible. The product was still launched in an area at that higher price, but soon had to be withdrawn because of very low sales. The research was repeated and again indicated that no price over 3p was possible, so the product was relaunched into other areas at 3p with reasonable sales results.

Another example shows how pricing research enabled a company to price a product at a much higher price than planned. A new drink went through a long evaluation and research programme and sales in a limited area were promising. Pricing research at this stage indicated that consumers could stand a much higher price, even 25 per cent more, and initial indications of sales at the higher price are most encouraging. Obviously such a difference in price has changed the profitability of the product out of all recognition.

It must also be pointed out that such pricing research need not be done in isolation on a new product; it can usually be combined with the usual hall and placement tests, so the research would cost little more.

Consumer durables present more of a problem, but nevertheless much can be done with photographs, or preferably, with prototypes, in order to obtain consumer reactions to the new product and the price. Moreover, if the purchase is really large and so of importance to the consumer, his reaction is likely to be even more precise and trustworthy than in the case of relatively trivial packaged goods.

Pricing decisions

Even if it is found that market research can give the company accurate information on which to make pricing decisions – and, whatever the attitudes towards the research, assumptions on the relationship between price and sales volume need to be made anyway – the process of decision on the pricing of new products is by no means straightforward.

Some companies have rigid rules instructing them to ensure that the new product is saddled with its rightful proportion of overheads in the same way as existing products. This approach does not take into account that the overheads already exist and certainly penalises the new product by forcing on it a price which is higher than would be warranted on a marginal profit basis.

Other companies have exactly the opposite outlook. They believe that the importance of new products is such that the existing products need to subsidise them and so no overheads of any kind are charged to them at any rate in the first few investment years. This approach can lead to unrealistically low costing if the company is willing to shut its eyes to the new product's overheads.

What is the answer? In my opinion the most useful approach in practice is well described in *Pricing for Profit and Growth* [12.9] where the authors argue rightly that it is a fallacy to consider that new products should be subject to full-costing and so should have a proper allocation of overheads on to them. What they should bear, however, is whatever it is estimated that they will add to the company's total current expenses, while they should not be charged with the actual development costs which must be allotted to the company's current operation in the development budget. Care needs to be taken, however, as it is too easy to use the marginal costing approach and there must be realism in forecasting what additional costs will be caused by the new product.

It may seem that these are details which will possibly change the price by only a minute amount. That is not so. They may not only affect the price but could also mean the difference between product failure and product success or between a decision to launch a product and one to kill it.

Let us look, for example, at hypothetical costings on a product which takes its 'rightful' share of overheads (Example A) as against the same product costed on extra total expenses it has led to (Example B) (see Table 12.1).

TABLE 12.1

	A	B
Retail selling price	15.0p	15.0p
Trade margins	3.8p	3.8p
Transport	0.8p	0.5p
Net sales revenue	10.4p	10.7p
Cost of goods	7.4p	7.4p
Gross profit	3.0p	3.3p
Sales force	0.7p	0.2p
Other overheads	0.9p	0.4p
Marketing	1.0p	1.0p
Net profit before tax	0.4p	1.7p

Example A assumes trade margins with allowance for quantity discounts at 25 per cent of retail selling price, transport at 7½ per cent, cost of goods at 71 per cent and fixed sales force and other overheads at 15 per cent of net sales revenue. In practice these are realistic figures on the basis of a total overhead allocation and if one adds 10 per cent for marketing the resulting 4 per cent for net profit looks poor if it is assumed that the above costings relate to the time when the new product is on a running basis, having passed the investment period.

How different are the results in Example B! The same assumptions have been used except that the extra transport costs added by the new product to the existing transport costs are taken to be 5 per cent. Likewise extra sales force and other overheads are also assumed to be only 6 per cent of net sales revenue. These seem reasonable assumptions, if, as so often happens, the existing sales force is used for the new product and distribution is through current outlets.

The net profit in Example B is over 16 per cent of net sales revenue – a fine achievement. In my experience, a project would normally be rejected on the profitability forecast in Example A and progressed with great excitement on the basis of the costing in Example B.

Another way of looking at the difference between the two projects in terms of price is to calculate that, to achieve the profit of Example B with retail selling price at 15p, the company would need to market the product at over 60p if it insists on using the costing procedure as shown in A. Thus a 300 per cent price rise would be necessary to pay for the company's refusal to accept marginal costing and such a rise can be high enough to put the project out of court again.

If the principle of marginal costing for new products is accepted and assumptions can be made on the relationship between prices and sales levels, the price decision should be

TABLE 12.2

1 Variable costs per unit, p	
Trade margins	3.8
Transport	0.5
Production	4.4
Sales force and other overheads	0.3
	9.0
2 Fixed costs at a volume of say 10 million units	
Plant and additional product personnel	3.0
Sales force and other overheads	0.3
Marketing	1.0
	4.3

based on study of the consequences of every possible pricing decision.

The costs will be divided into:

1 Variable costs.
2 Fixed costs.

The variable costs will include the production costs for each unit of the product and the selling and distribution costs which will vary in direct relationship to the sales volume.

The fixed costs will include marketing expenditure, additional labour taken on to be engaged specifically in the operation and capital costs of the plant depreciated over its estimated economic life and allowing at the same time for obsolescence.

It follows that, within a certain volume bracket, the fixed costs will not change until, for example, the point has been reached where new overheads, such as the building of a new factory, are incurred.

Thus, if fixed costs are constant in the defined volume bracket, the price estimated to yield the highest gross contribution from the variable costs is the most profitable price for the new product.

TABLE 12.3 Profitability estimates at different prices

Price	12p	13p	14p	15p	16p	17p	18p	19p
Sales volume, million units	16	13	11	10	8	6	5	4
Gross contribution per unit before fixed costs (variable cost = 9.0p/unit), p	3.0	4.0	5.0	6.0	7.0	8.0	9.0	10.0
Gross contribution before fixed costs, £'000	480	520	550	600	560	480	450	400
Fixed costs, £'000	430	430	430	430	430	430	430	430
Net profit before tax, £'000	50	90	120	170	130	50	20	-30

If the example already used is applied here on the B costings divided into fixed and variable costs it is assumed that the breakdown would be as shown in Table 12.2.

If the fixed costs are applied to a volume of 10 million units, their total annual cost will be £430,000.

It is now possible to build up a table covering the estimated annual profitability during the economic life of the product and at different price levels. Let us assume that if the product is priced at between 12p and 19p the resulting sales volume estimates will be as shown in Table 12.3. On the basis of this table, 15p per unit is the most profitable price. Even if the sales volume forecasts at different prices can only be very rough, it is felt that such an exercise as described here provides a useful basis for pricing and is not used by companies often enough.

Once the cost estimates are broken down into fixed and variable, the rest of the exercise is extremely simple.

13 Market research for new products

Need for normative data

Market research in various aspects plays an important part in the development of new products and is mentioned often throughout the book. Yet it is sad to reflect that one cannot really take advantage of all the research experience which has been collected over the years. Every day a number of new product surveys are being carried out and yet, when a company embarks on one, it needs to start from scratch as if none of the other companies' research had taken place.

Naturally an individual piece of research is confidential to the company for whom it has been done, but I take the research industry to task for not having established any procedure for aggregating results so that everyone can benefit from the general experience. One exception is the Nielsen Company who show what can be done by studying the general conclusions arising from their retail audits and publishing the trends regularly in the *Nielsen Researcher* both in the US and in the UK. Another is Andrew Ehrenberg who has done much pioneering work in this area, but it is a shame that few others have imitated them in this respect.

For example, study of a large number of surveys in many fields should lead to general conclusions showing certain relationships between different factors. It may be possible to relate preference in a blind product test to a subsequent market share; or the proportion of people saying they would buy a product to the number actually buying; or advertising awareness to consumer trial or shop distribution to knowledge of the product.

In some cases it may be impossible to draw any general conclusions and so the argument behind which we shield ourselves when asked about such general principles: 'it all depends' is right. I am convinced, however, that very important relationships can be established which would make marketing more scientific and so, hopefully, more profitable.

Until some central organisation is set up to cope with the problem, the company must collect its own data bank. Even the biggest users of research will not be able to reach entirely satisfactory conclusions because the research is likely to have been confined to a narrow number of fields, but even so it is worth trying to study what information the company can collect from its files. It can be very much better than nothing and yet very few companies seem to think such an approach worth while.

For example, a middle-sized consumer goods company, operating in a number of markets linked with each other, recently collected all the data it had from just six test markets in its product field. Consumer research and retail audits had been conducted in each case, so it was possible to see if there was any relationship between the weight of marketing expenditure, the levels of brand awareness, consumer trial and consumer sales. Interestingly, even the very modest number of six test markets produced a general pattern which proved invaluable when another test market was planned in a similar product field.

In the same way most medium-sized and large companies have a mass of past market research data in their files. However rough and difficult to compare, it can still provide useful guidance to those planning more research on new products.

Perhaps the day will come when we shall all know on the basis of 40,000 surveys that a new product achieving a 60:40 preference over the brand leader in a blind product test has a 75 per cent chance of obtaining at least half the brand leader's sales in the first year of marketing. Until that happy day comes – and I doubt that it ever will – companies must seek their normative data as well as they can. Such past research is worth its weight in gold.

Use of research

I am sorry if I often sound a critical note against the way in which market research is often used in new product development, but I feel that all too frequently it is conducted for its own sake and not with the company's profits in mind. For example, if a company is interested in a specific product field, it is too easy to decide that it is necessary to know immediately everything about it. A mammoth operation is mounted to check on consumer usage and attitudes, volumes of tables are produced and over £10,000 can easily be spent. A company needs only to be mildly interested in twenty markets to spend £200,000 or more on very broad and not particularly helpful research.

There is a danger of spending too much on market research in development, just as it is dangerous to spend too little. It may seem a cliché, but the justification of a piece of research should be in terms of the financial return likely to be derived from it and compared with the decisions which would need to be taken without market research information.

I am a strong supporter, therefore, of regarding the use of market research in the development process as a bit by bit operation, on the same principles as the step by step development process of a new product which has been already described.

Thus instead of the proverbial £5000-£10,000 large survey at the start of the operation, it seems far more beneficial to start off by collecting all the desk research which may include published market research data. A small piece of research costing only £1000-£1200 could follow to give the company a feel of the market, even if it can be hardly quantified on the basis of such research. If the project is still viable, it may then be advisable to find out further information on one specific aspect, following the previous research, and say £2000-£3000 could be spent at this stage. Again the project would re-evaluated and, if it passes the test, further research may be necessary costing now, perhaps, £5000-£6000.

Altogether it is possible that the company finishes up by spending more by adopting the type of system described above than if it had undertaken one large survey at the beginning. This assumes, however, that the project progresses through the various stages to justify all the pieces of research one after another. In practice a number of projects will be eliminated early, so the limitation of research expenditure at the beginning should lead to savings.

Secondly, in a multi-stage research operation the company

learns from one stage to the next, so the research incorporates the lessons arising from the preceding work and answers the specific questions raised by the previous research. The final results therefore should be much more useful than those of a single survey at the outset of the operation.

Moreover, there is general reluctance to use crude forms of fact finding, if the finances of a project do not warrant anything else at that stage. For example, telephone research or postal research may not be ideal and certainly good arguments can be advanced against them. They should not be spurned, however, as if research technique were some sacrosanct factor in the development process.

For example, a small number of questions among upper and middle class women could easily be asked by telephone or telephone-owning housewives. Or reactions towards a consumer durable can be obtained by means of a postal questionnaire among past buyers of the product. In such cases, where the respondent is interested in the subject, response rates of even 80 per cent have been recorded in postal surveys.

So let us not scorn research methods which at times may seem cheap and nasty. Even such pieces of research have a role to play in new product development.

Concept research

In theory it appears possible to conduct a market survey into a market to discover consumer characteristics and attitudes and to find gaps in the market which can lead to a suitable product concept. In practice, however, it has already been mentioned that such an approach tends to be not very fruitful, simply because the public finds it difficult or impossible in most markets to express any desire for new products.

Similarly, the problem exists in a group discussion, although it is then possible for an experienced discussion leader to direct the conversation into specific areas. In general the consumer thinks very narrowly about a market and the products in it. His or her terms of reference are naturally the existing products which are usually satisfactory and any suggestions for new products tend to be extremely close to the existing one [13.1].

The experience mentioned above refers particularly to fast-moving packaged goods. In consumer durables where an item costs a considerable amount of money and purchase follows careful evaluation by the consumer, it is likely that knowledge of existing products can be high and so suggestions for product improvements and completely new innovations could result.

It is noteworthy that Massey Ferguson claims to start its process of new product development with market research [13.2]. Similarly continuous consumer attitude studies in cars, TV sets, washing machines, etc. among buyers of both the company's and the competitor's products could well be fruitful. It is important, however, for the company to be happy that the consumers are really interested and knowledgeable enough to talk usefully about a product field, if such research is to be undertaken.

Unless, therefore, there are likely to be very clear cut consumer suggestions for new products, it is better for them to come from the company as a result of internal concept search methods. Then it is most fruitful to ask the consumer for reactions towards the suggested concepts.

Even so the concepts, unless extremely simple, are not easy to grasp in an abstract form and it is advisable to be able to show a physical representation in the form of a product or a rough prototype or even in the form of an illustration, possibly as part of an advertisement.

Once there is something concrete which can be shown to the consumer, which requires comment on an idea rather than a long leap into the unknown, he is often extremely helpful in reacting either in individual depth interviews or in group discussions. It is certainly possible to go some way to validation of a concept through the use of such methods, although what cannot be done with any precision is to quantify the importance of the concept and so find out how much the consumer is willing to pay for it in practice. This can only be found to some extent in the subsequent quantitative research and, more accurately, in the market place.

Product testing

For many years up to the late 1960s, wherever possible a product was given to the consumer 'blind' i.e. unidentified, to be compared with a popular competitive product already on the market, which of course was also tested blind. If the new product won or at any rate showed no strong negatives, then it could be assumed that it was worth going on to the next stage. In the case of durables it was necessary to use prototypes from which reactions were obtained.

In practice, product research, though it sounds simple, raises certain problems which can be listed as follows:

1 What factors should be included in the comparison between the two products and what importance should be given to each one? The consumer may prefer one product on certain grounds and the other on others and it is also possible that the most important points of distinction between the two products, as far as the consumer is concerned, are not listed at all in the questionnaire.

It is useful, therefore, to predetermine, whether from research information or on judgement, the most important consumer factors in the particular market and their relative importance. On this basis, and subject to any changes arising from the actual concept of the new product, it should be possible to include the important factors, while knowledge of their relative importance would be vital at the interpretative stage.

2 The results of a quick test can be very different from what would happen in practice over a considerable time span. For example, a company testing a new snack product against an established one found that the former had good comparative acceptance when a small portion of both products was eaten. The project went on to a test market, but there it was found that the test results had been misleading because the new product, though palatable in small doses, palled when eaten in large quantities and over a longer period. Similarly it is well known that in a small product test Acid Spangles were the most popular variety because of their strong flavour, but over a period more neutral varieties would in fact sell much better because Acid Spangles can be eaten in small doses, but not in large quantities.

If it is suspected that this problem could arise, it is important to give the consumer a large quantity of the product or to repeat the test a number of times at close intervals.

3 Absence of strong negatives does not reflect any positive feelings. It is possible for a product to arouse little or no unfavourable comment, but later the product can still perform badly in the market place, if it does not offer any strong positive advantage.

4 In many packaged goods, the product is only a small part of the product as bought by the consumer. Thus beans in tomato sauce would achieve quite a different reaction from Heinz Baked Beans.

Interpretation of the product testing can be a problem. It is also possible that the new product, although well behind the competitor overall, scores particularly well with a segment of the sample, so that narrow appeal to a sector of the market could be a possibility.

For this reason it is useful, when market segmentation is a possibility, to use a much bigger sample than is usual for product testing, in order to see whether preference for the new product is strong in a particular subsample, even if it is weak overall.

Despite the problems in the product testing of consumer goods, the risks are still not too great because the company can go on to later stages such as tests in a number of shops or in a test town or a larger area to obtain further indications of consumer reaction. In the case of consumer durables this is often not possible, so the product testing stage is much more crucial, being nearer to the eventual final steps in the decision process regarding the product.

At the same time, it is very rare for a completely new concept to be introduced in durables, so a manufacturer normally has as a useful starting point a wealth of data on consumer reactions towards existing products. For example, a car manufacturer [13.3] faced with continuous need to introduce new models could well conduct continuous research on attitudes towards their cars among car owners – Mr Leyshon mentions a company conducting three-monthly surveys – to build up a background against which to introduce new models.

Naturally, it is again crucial to establish the relative importance of each factor and it is not easy to realise that in a product with a high engineering and design content the consumer could be particularly influenced by, say, the door locks of a car.

Because of its great importance in the development process, the product testing of durables is itself protracted over a number of stages as the product becomes developed. Thus, in the case of a car, consumer attitudes could first be sought towards an illustration, then a clay model mock up, then say a fibre-glass mo el and finally a sheet-metal one, the reactions to each step enabli the company to revise the model and test it at the next stage.

Timing is naturally an important factor in the development of a new durable, the gestation period of a new durable being longer than that of an elephant. Leyshon quotes four years for a car as an average period from the initial sketches to the production model and the product research could well be stretched out over most of that time.

In recent years, marketing men in packaged goods have realised more and more the need to test the concept as well as the package. This, of course, is what developing brands is all about [13.4]. In practice the easiest way to cater for this is to develop a concept visually and in physical form if possible, so that consumers are shown both a representation of the product and a rough pack or concept board showing the brand name and the main selling points. The initial research is likely to take the form of group discussions covering a large number of concepts. The best ones are then developed further and are tested quantitatively, consumers being given the products to use at home where relevant.

The approach thus combines reactions to the product itself with those to its 'image'. Detailed pricing questions can also be combined with the product testing, but in my experience, one or two questions such as what price does the consumer expect to pay or would he/she buy at one particular price are not enough. The Gabor/Granger approach is much preferable.

Other forms of research

Other types of research are used, as already mentioned, in the development process, to assist in the naming, procing, packaging, advertising, test marketing, etc. More details are to be found under the appropriate chapters.

14 The trade

Reaction to new products

There is an attitude among certain companies, particularly the larger ones and those heavily oriented towards the consumer, that the trade are not particularly important in the new product development process. If the product seems to meet the company criteria in the planning stages and if it has a consumer advantage over the competition, then surely the trade will be no problem. They will simply funnel the product from the company to the consumer and this will in the process benefit them as well.

This reasoning may be plausible, in theory, but does not always work in practice, because the trade have become an increasingly important factor. Whereas even in the early 1960s any well known company launching a new product could guarantee a sterling distribution level of, say, 60 per cent in grocers and up to 90 per cent in chemists, the situation has since become much more difficult. In the 1970s the same company would be delighted with 40-45 per cent in grocery outlets.

The concentration of power among the trade into fewer and larger groups and the consequent general increase in scientific methods in retailing has led to a notable decline in stock levels and particularly in the number of brands stocked. For example a chain of multiple grocers, who at one time would have stocked six or seven brands in a market of any size, now tend to stock the brand leader, their own label and possibly one other brand as an alternative. To persuade the retailer to add to those three needs either an extremely attractive and so unprofitable offer or a product with such superiority over the competition that the sceptical buyer will accept it on that basis alone.

N. H. Borden [14.1] shows in his US study how buying

committees reacted to a salesman's presentation of a new product introduction. In many cases the haphazard nature of the decision whether to stock it or not was astonishing. Decisions were made very quickly – one in thirty seconds – there were no specific buying criteria and only in one case among the many quoted was any consideration given to the effect on inventory. Even so only a small proportion of new products were accepted in the US supermarkets at that time.

It is likely that buying decisions have recently become more scientific both in the United States and in Britain, even if there is doubtless a proportion of buyers in buying committees who are behaving very amateurishly. However the buyer behaves, the odds must be against the new product, on the one hand because of conservatism and on the other on the basis of financial reasoning, e.g. to cut down stocks. This aspect has become increasingly relevant in the economic difficulties of the 1970s [14.2].

It is important, therefore, and it is becoming increasingly so, that the company should consider carefully the likely reaction of the trade to a new product launch and should prepare its presentation to the trade meticulously. It pays.

Variation in trade attitudes

The trade by themselves can make or break a new product and yet this point is not always appreciated when one attempts to make the invariably difficult analysis of reasons why some products fail and others succeed. It also seems that the trade have different attitudes to different companies which have an important bearing on the trade attitudes to new products.

There are some companies, for example, which are particularly unpopular with the trade who are nevertheless forced to stock existing brands. Yet it is much easier to find reasons against accepting their new products if possible, whereas sympathy is extended at times to small companies. This could explain why there have been surprising examples of successful new products launched by small companies competing with much larger ones.

It also seems that the trade regard companies in a certain context and so look on their new products with favour if they are in some fields but not in others. For example, two large companies recently launched similar toiletry ranges in the same area. One achieved immediately very high distribution, while the other found it almost impossible to have any at all, the main difference being that the latter was not regarded by the trade as a toiletry company. Similarly another recently launched a product that has been most successful for only one reason. It was exactly the same product as that of the brand leader, but the latter was very unpopular with the trade who, for once, welcomed the 'me-too' product with open arms. On the other hand, another recent new product was victimised by some buyers because it was a food product produced by the subsidiary of a chemical company and the buyers felt strongly that food and chemicals should not go together!

If it is accepted that the trade are vital in a new product launch and that they will react to a new product in different ways, according to their views of the company marketing it, it follows that each company must not only cultivate the trade but must also find out whether the trade regard them as particularly suitable to market products in some markets and not in others. Such trade enquiries prove normally to be extremely useful. Even if the company may still decide that it has such a good proposition that it will persuade the trade to accept a product from them in what seems an unsuitable product field, nevertheless it is important to assess beforehand the level of acceptance or of resistance which is likely to be offered.

Because of the lack of published information on trade attitudes, I have been very involved in studies of the UK grocery retail trade [14.3]. These have shown that grocers have a reasonably favourable attitude to new products, and of some companies who have a poor trade record in this area. Interestingly in each of the three surveys 47 companies were given ratings by the trade on their new product record and a number of famous international companies, including some from the United States, languished consistently at the bottom of the list. Some of the more interesting findings are shown in Table 14.1. Some of the answers may not be related to actual practice, but they indicate nevertheless the increasing sophistication of the retailer. This has been felt even by an enormous international grocery manufacturer who sent a special accounts

TABLE 14.1

Number of new products offered in average month	%	Percentage accepted	%
Under 5	16	Under 15%	50
5 - 20	61	15 - 29	27
20 - 40	15	30 - 49	13
40 - 60	6	50 - 69	9
Over 60	2	Over 70	1

Main reasons for acceptance	%	For refusal	%
Strong advertising	72	Poor quality	66
Good product quality	68	Little advertising	57
Well known company	61	No product plans	56
Bonus	37	Declining market	51
Product advantages	27	No shelf space	39
Well tested	24	No bonus	25
Other	5	Small company	7
		Other	10

Is attitude to new product strongly affected by company concerned?	%	Basis for measuring success of new product	%
Yes	65	Profitability/ft^2	71
No	34	Expansion of total category	54
Don't know	1	Market share	52
		Suitability for display	27
		Effect on own label	13
		Other	10

executive to sell in a new product and was met by a detailed questionnaire requesting details of previous product and test market research. As very little had been done, to save time the company was forced to go back to do its homework!

Yet it is possible to obtain reasonable distribution for new products as shown by research conducted in October/November 1974 [14.4] (see Table 14.2). All these products in very

TABLE 14.2 Sterling distribution

	Multiples only, %	All grocers, %
Procter & Gamble's Head and Shoulders Shampoo	82	68
Brooke Bond Brazilian Coffee	78	56
Beecham's Aquafresh Toothpaste	59	51
Petfood's Cupboard Love	57	45
Quaker Felix Tender Morsels	62	43
Kellogg's Country Store	53	42

competitive markets, seemed to have quickly achieved good distribution, especially in all the important multiples. The trade play fair and tend to give the manufacturer a chance; it is up to the manufacturer to take the chance.

Marketing support

The need to have an important product advantage has already been mentioned, so that the trade should have good justification for stocking.

Another particularly important factor is the marketing support which the new product will be given. In fact in Borden's enquiry in the United States it was apparent that the product by itself was not considered particularly important by the trade. More important was the marketing programme supporting it and, at least in some cases, the buying committee accepted a product solely because of the marketing support. I had a similar experience when selling a new product to chemist wholesalers in the UK. Before I could describe the product, I was asked whether it was going to be on television and, when they heard that it would be, the buyers immediately expressed interest without even knowing what the product was!

At the same time there can be a difference between promise and performance. Naturally a company must put its marketing programme in the most favourable light, but even so many companies have done themselves a disservice through ridiculous exaggeration.

For example, if a company intends to spend on advertising, say, £30,000 over three months in an area representing 25 per cent of the country, there is a strong temptation to calculate the equivalent national expenditure over twelve months and to announce a very strong advertising campaign of £500,000 without being too particular about explaining this figure. And this is the kind of a temptation to which some well-known companies have succumbed in the past.

Similarly, even a casual examination of advertisements in trade publications will show extraordinary promises. They claim that hundreds of millions of people will be reached by the campaign, presumably multiplying actual coverage by the estimated frequency of this coverage. Or hundreds and even thousands of television spots are mentioned, so that if there are 50 spots in each of the 8 areas the spurious total becomes 400 spots! It is also by no means unknown for promised campaigns to disintegrate mysteriously after a few weeks, although of course a company has every right and indeed a duty to its shareholders to cut expenditure which is proving unprofitable.

It is not surprising therefore, that the trade are sceptical of such promises of support, particularly if they have been caught out a number of times. So even if a company benefits once or twice by persuading the trade to stock and display a new product to a degree which is completely out of proportion with the product potential and its marketing programme, in the long term the company's approach must rebound against it. It must be expected, therefore, that some companies who always match promise with performance have established better trade relations than others who appear to have let the trade down at times. Companies would do well to appreciate this factor, as many have done already.

It is also worth noting the type of marketing support which the trade appreciate particularly. As far as advertising is concerned, every survey published on the subject shows that in the case of product groups for which television is applicable a dominant majority of the trade believe it to be more effective than other media. This attitude has been confirmed whenever I have had an opportunity of talking to the trade on this subject.

The trade attitude does not mean, of course, that television must be used for every new product, but the trade factor should at any rate be considered when the advertising media are chosen. Moreover it is sometimes advisable to devote part of the budget to co-operative advertising with the trade. This works particularly well if the trade consists of a small number of outlets where support is particularly important, e.g. in the case of a new motor car or of a new type of holiday. In both markets the local outlet – garage or travel agent – has a considerable influence on the customer in an advisory capacity, so a close link in the promotion between retailer and manufacturer is likely to be beneficial. There is also a trend in packaged goods towards exclusive promotions with the large and increasingly powerful multiple chains and again these could be used for new products, especially in order to obtain distribution in the chain concerned.

The economics of below-the-line expenditure, i.e. trade and consumer promotions, needs in fact to be considered carefully in the launch of a new product. Their growing importance in most markets coupled with the prevalent abolition of resale price maintenance has led to a considerable amount of pressure by the trade on manufacturers. The amount devoted to trade margins and special discounts has been growing generally and in some cases, particularly in certain packaged goods markets, the manufacturers have found themselves in a very difficult position. Finding perhaps that a trade bonus led to a sales increase, a company would repeat it. The competition would then follow with a higher bonus and over the years the market would become one dominated by trade bonuses, hardly any product being sold to the trade at its full price. Thus there are companies with sales forces which believe that they cannot sell without very heavy trade bonuses, so that there are expenditures of even £500,000 on trade promotion and only £100,000 on consumer advertising. Such circumstances have also led to very strong pressure on manufacturers' margins and some companies have even become bankrupt directly because of this reason.

It is not easy for a company to break away from the pressure on trade discounts for its existing products, once it has opened the door in this way. It is possible, however, to change the situation as far as new products are concerned by taking a strong position from the beginning, and companies have found in fact that they have been able to maintain their trade prices on new products even though they continue to give away part of their margins on the established ones.

Thus the company must reconcile its desire for good trade relations with the need for a strong attitude on trade discounts. In practice this is not as difficult a problem as it may appear at first. Refusal to limit trade discounts is a sign of strength and would even lead to more respect by the trade towards the particular company.

This does not mean that trade discounts can be eliminated completely for a new product. They are the established method for obtaining initial distribution and should certainly be used in the first journey cycle, as long as it is made very clear to the trade that the first journey is a special occasion and that the discount will not be repeated. On the subsequent calls the sales force must in fact resist the temptation of giving further discounts and instead the company should concentrate on consumer promotion in the form of advertising, sampling, couponing, competitions and any other method of stimulating consumer demand. A strong sales force should be able to persuade the trade that it is in the interest of the latter as well as of the company to concentrate all expenditure to persuade the consumer to buy from the retail outlet.

The marketing plans for the new product should provide, therefore, for a strong pricing policy and for the bulk of the expenditure to be devoted to stimulation of consumer demand.

Presentation to the trade

As a few buyers are not so important in a new product introduction, it follows that much attention needs to be given to the method whereby the company presents the new product to these buyers. This means not only the proverbial launching party, but also the occasion when the company faces the buyer and needs to persuade him to stock and promote the new product.

There has already been a trend in some companies to form a small sales force of senior sales executives to look after the large buyers only. In many cases it is also likely to be profitable to build up a detailed presentation for these buyers. After all, if the company has gone through the development process up to test market or a launch, the evidence of the opportunity in the market and the suitability of the product to exploit this opportunity should be as relevant to the trade as it is to the company. If the company had not thought that there would be good reasons for the trade to accept the product, they would not have gone ahead.

There are also accounts when an individually prepared presentation could be justified despite the high cost which this would usually entail. There is a moral in the story of one company launching a new product, which prepared a very elaborate presentation to be used specifically for one account. After the presentation, the company's managing director exploded when he saw the bill for its preparation and threatened to refuse to authorise payment. When, however, news came through of the order received as a result of the presentation, the managing director immediately forgot his threats. It had been well worth the expense.

There must be many such cases where an elaborate presentation, possibly incorporating exclusive promotional deals for a large buyer, will justify the effort and expenditure involved.

Importance of company to the trade

A company's importance to the trade depends largely on two factors:

1 Its size.
2 Its range of products.

As competition grows, so the size of a company becomes increasingly important in dealing with the trade. A large company with a wide spread of products should be in a stronger negotiating position, other things being equal, than a small company in the same field. In fact as the trade are bound to continue their policy of stock rationalisation, it must follow that it is the small company's products which will tend to be cut out, unless there are specific reasons for not doing so, while the large company's products will take over.

It follows that companies, if they want to survive, will need to include in their planning provisions to grow to the required size to make them important to their particular trade buyers. Some mergers can only be explained if the main purpose was growth to a unit of a certain size rather than short-term profits.

Similarly, the company needs to consider the importance to the trade of the product range it offers. Even large international companies can have built up their turnover on peripheral products and they are likely to be vulnerable in the long term against competitors who also market more essential very high volume products which must be stocked by the trade.

A number of companies have already realised how vital it will become in the future to have in their range products which will be important enough to the trade to maintain distribution for the other products too. In fact the addition to the existing company range of one or more products which will open the door for their sales force as 'lead lines' can easily be one of the objectives in the company's development policy. For example, an international company made a very large acquisition in the UK which has been much criticised for being unprofitable in the short term. The main objective of the acquisition, however, was to add to the company's power in the long term and the combination of the two companies will have an important range of products and considerable negotiating strength in the future. On the basis of these criteria the acquisition has been a great success.

It is also possible that a number of packaged-goods companies which have developed in the convenience area, particularly in the last few years, will think again. Convenience products have proved vulnerable to economic recession, both in the USA and UK. I can see a move by some companies back to commodity products that can represent large and stable opportunities.

Me, buy a dishwasher?
No thanks!
They're difficult to load.
They don't get the dishes really clean.
They're far too big
and expensive.
Not any more, Madam!
The all-new KIM dishwasher has been developed by the precision-minded Swiss to fit real-life kitchens. It loads from the front in exactly one minute. It gets dishes, glasses, cups, knives, forks and spoons, whistling, shiny, clean . . . spotlessly dry. And it costs just 69 gns.
They have finally perfected dishwashers.
At last it makes sense for you to be free from the miserable and messy chore of continual washing up. The new KIM dishwasher, after heating the water, will wash and dry the dishes, cups and cutlery used by six people in eight and a half minutes! And – hold your breath – it will do them as thoroughly and as efficiently as you could do them yourself, even more hygienically.
Designed for real-life kitchens. The new KIM is truly a table-model dishwasher. The base measures exactly 19½ inches by 19½ inches. It does not have to be plumbed in. (No installation charges.) It sits with beautiful compactness on top of your draining board or working surface or, if you prefer, on its own 'working space' trolley. It uses the tap in your sink (cold or hot water) for about a minute before you press the button; the tap is then free.
KIM is completely automatic. Here is what you do: Load the dishes, cups, glasses and cutlery into their own specially cushioned slots. Slide the single rack back into the machine. Close the door. Turn on the tap for a minute. Press the button.
Here is what KIM does: Heats the water to 150°F. Mixes in a special detergent. Washes each piece perfectly with a powerful curtain of water. (Only the water moves.) Rinses everything with fresh, hot, clean water. Dries contents to a bright shine. Empties the water into your sink. Shuts itself off.
KIM is more hygienic. KIM uses steaming water to wash up – water at a temperature no human hand could bear yet gentle enough for your most delicate glass. KIM uses only clean water for the rinse. And you need never use a tea towel on your family's dishes again.
KIM is simplicity itself. The ingenious Swiss have "transistorised" dishwashers. They have managed to eliminate all the unnecessary bulk and trim (which has tended to make dishwashers so expensive) and have developed a precision-minded marvel that is simplicity itself. That's why KIM, the new fully-automatic dishwasher, costs just 69 gns. (Or after a down payment of £7.9.0 you pay 24 monthly payments of £3.5.0 each.)
About the makers of KIM. It took five long years of design, research and testing to develop a dishwasher as practical as KIM. The people responsible are Switzerland's largest manufacturers of fully automatic washing machines and dishwashers. KIM dishwashers are now being manufactured in Britain and are being serviced within hours of your call by a large force of fully-trained British engineers. KIM is completely guaranteed for one year – both parts and labour!
Seeing is believing. KIM is available from the manufacturer. A comprehensive booklet has been prepared which tries to answer any question you can possibly dream up. It shows you KIM in operation. The booklet is yours free for the asking. Unless you are in love with the idea of washing up for the rest of your life, why not write now. You'll be glad you did.
Kim
Automatic
Dishwasher
Kim Engineering Limited, Dept. E, 11 Clifford Street, London, W.1.
Please send me your free brochure about the revolutionary KIM dishwasher.
Or Telephone: Birmingham CENtral 1794 Ext. 228 (day or night).
Name
(please use block capitals)
Address
Postal District
County

Plate I Advertisement A

"Me, buy a dishwasher?
No thanks!
They're difficult to load . . . they don't get the dishes really clean . . . and they're far too big and expensive."
NOT ANY MORE, MADAM!
The all-new KIM Dishwasher has been developed by the precision-minded Swiss to fit real-life kitchens. It loads from the front in exactly one minute. It gets dishes, glasses, cups, knives, forks and spoons, whistling, shiny, clean . . . spotlessly dry. And it costs just 69 gns.
They have finally perfected dishwashers. At last it makes sense for you to be free from the miserable and messy chore of continual washing-up.
The new KIM dishwasher, after heating the water, will wash and dry the dishes, glasses, cups and cutlery used by six people in eight and a half minutes! And – hold your breath – it will do them as thoroughly and as efficiently as you could do them yourself, even more hygienically.
Designed for real-life kitchens. The new KIM is truly a table-model dishwasher. It measures exactly 19½ inches by 19½ inches. It does not have to be plumbed in. (No installation charges.) It sits with beautiful compactness on top of your draining board or working surface or, if you prefer, on its own 'working space' trolley. It uses the tap in your sink (cold or hot water) for about a minute before you press the button; the tap is then free.
KIM is completely automatic. Here is what you do: Load the dishes, cups, glasses and cutlery into their own specially cushioned slots. Slide the single rack back into the machine. Close the door. Turn on the tap for a minute. Press the button. Here is what KIM does: Heats the water to 150°F. Mixes in a special detergent. Washes each piece perfectly with a powerful curtain of water. (Only the water moves.) Rinses everything with fresh, hot, clean water. Dries contents to a bright shine. Empties the water into your sink. Shuts itself off.
KIM is more hygienic. KIM uses steaming water to wash up – water at a temperature no human hand could bear yet gentle enough for your most delicate glass. KIM uses only clean water for the rinse. And you need never use a tea towel on your family's dishes again.
KIM is simplicity itself. The ingenious Swiss have "transistorised" dishwashers. They have managed to eliminate all the unnecessary bulk and trim (which has tended to make dishwashers so expensive) and have developed a precision-minded marvel that is simplicity itself. That's why KIM, the new fully-automatic dishwasher, costs just 69 gns. (Or after a down payment of £7.9.0 you pay 24 monthly payments of £3.5.0 each.)
About the makers of KIM. It took five long years of design, research and testing to develop a dishwasher as practical as KIM. The people responsible are Switzerland's largest manufacturers of fully automatic washing machines and dishwashers. KIM dishwashers are now being manufactured in Britain and are being serviced within hours of your call by a large force of fully-trained British engineers. KIM is completely guaranteed for one year – both parts and labour!
Seeing is believing. KIM is available from the manufacturer. A comprehensive booklet has been prepared which tries to answer any question you can possibly dream up. It shows you KIM in operation. The booklet is yours free for the asking. Unless you are in love with the idea of washing up for the rest of your life, why not write now. You'll be glad you did.
SEND FOR FREE
QUESTION-ANSWERING BROCHURE
KIM ENGINEERING LIMITED
Dept. A, 11 Clifford Street, London W.1
or telephone
LONDON: GERrard 8475 Ext. 656
BIRMINGHAM: CENtral 1796 Ext. 250
BRISTOL: 674431 Ext. A
MANCHESTER: CENtral 6566 Ext. 217
NAME
ADDRESS
Postal District
County
kim
FULLY AUTOMATIC
DISHWASHER
69
GNS

Plate II Advertisement B

15 Marketing expenditure

Need for brand promotion

New consumer product launches are normally accompanied by large expenditure on marketing and one wonders at times whether this is always justified. Would it perhaps be more profitable for the company to let the product, if good enough, speak for itself? I know that such thoughts are anathema to the modern marketing approach, but hang the theoretical approach if there is more profit elsewhere.

In fact in most cases a company does need to spend on marketing and particularly on brand promotion for two main reasons:

1 To establish an identity for the new product which will help it both against existing products and against future competitors.

2 To fight the 'own brands'.

The first point is obvious and naturally important. At the same time a company could launch a new product very cheaply by producing it for a retail organisation rather than marketing it by itself. Such a policy could be attractive in the short term or for a small company without resources for branded marketing, but which at the same time desires to retain its independence.

Such a policy would be indeed shortsighted, however. Own brands have increased in importance in recent years, especially in packaged goods where in many cases they represent up to 20-25 per cent of the total market, and it is likely that they will continue to expand if the US experience is to be repeated.

Own brand business represents useful marginal profit for the large consumer goods manufacturers, but it also provides a very important reason for launching branded products as well. Only the latter provide any security for the company by forcing the trade to stock them if they establish a consumer franchise which the own brands cannot satisfy.

Once the company accepts the need for marketing expenditure to support a new product launch, it is necessary to decide the level of this expenditure. Yet, however extraordinary it may appear, there is not any accepted way of deciding this level. There seems to be no method which can even begin to claim that it is scientific despite the frequency with which such decisions need to be made by so many companies.

A study completed by the Marketing Society [15.1] reviewed current methods of setting advertising and marketing appropriations, and serious objections were raised in all cases.

Basically three main factors need to be considered in this connection:

1 The market type.
2 The required market share.
3 The competition.

If the market is ripe for considerable expansion, the current expenditure need not be considered too closely as the company will probably want to spend at a much higher rate to capture the lion's share of the expanded market. If, on the other hand, the aim is to enter a developed market and to obtain volume for the new product at the expense of the companies in the market rather than from market expansion, then very close attention will certainly need to be paid to what is happening in the market currently.

The degree of brand loyalty in the market will obviously affect the level of the appropriation. There are some markets, e.g. shampoos and other hair products such as hairsprays or colourants, which thrive on variety as the consumer is always anxious to try a new product. By contrast there are other markets, e.g. bread, where the consumer is extremely conservative and so there are very few new product introductions.

It follows, therefore, that the marketing effort in a fickle market needs to be relatively smaller at the outset than in a conservative one and the expenditure will need to be concentrated on the stages after the launch to ensure that initial consumer trial is translated into the required rate of repeat and regular purchasing. The conservative markets, on the other hand, will tend to require a very high level of expenditure just to break into the market and obtain consumer trial.

If this is achieved the follow-up stages leading to regular purchasing probably require less effort and expenditure than in the fickle markets.

Even after the company has established clearly the characteristics of the market which it intends to enter, the relationship between market share and marketing expenditure still needs to be calculated and informed guesswork or 'intuition' is the main basis for decision. Nielsen [15.2] have analysed new products in packaged goods and have concluded, on the basis of detailed study of such new products, that on average a new product in its first two years needed to spend on advertising at twice the rate of the established competition in the product field. Thus, in order to obtain a market share of 10 per cent in a developed market, the new product would need to have 20 per cent of the marketing expenditure.

As a rule of thumb such a ratio is reasonable because in most cases the new product must spend at a rate considerably higher than the average in the market in order to be noticed and to break through as well as to combat the marketing effort which the established companies have accumulated over the years. Thus a new entrant into, say, domestic appliances would need normally to spend extremely heavily to compensate for the millions of pounds which have made names such as Hoover and Hotpoint well known and respected by both the trade and the public.

At the same time, it must be noted that in the Nielsen study there are large variations around the average and that some successful new products were introduced at no more than the average rate in the market. The quality of the marketing effort and the degree to which the new product has clear advantages over the existing ones are both factors which need to be taken into account.

One recent new product succeeded despite very modest support whereas another introduction in the same market by a very large company backed by expenditure at five times the rate of the former product was a complete failure. The main difference was in the quality of the marketing, the smaller expenditure being used unquestionably much more effectively than the large one.

If the product has very strong advantages over the competition, it is possible to spend relatively little just to demonstrate the advantage so long as there is no need to pre-empt possible competition for the advanced product. Thus Turtle Wax quickly established itself as a leading car polish with relatively little marketing expenditure. Similarly Wilkinson Sword obtained a large share of the razor blade market with their stainless blade again with fairly small marketing expenditure which later needed to be raised very considerably because of competition from Gillette.

It is useful also to attack the expenditure problem from the other end, i.e. to decide what needs to be done and then consider how much is necessary to do it. In this way one will avoid the danger of reaching an expenditure level which makes sense in relation to the market and the competition, but none at all in absolute terms. For example, a company intending to enter a market of £4 million at retail selling price in which total marketing expenditure is £250,000 may conclude quite reasonably that it should obtain an average share of 10 per cent in the first two years by spending no more than £60,000 -£70,000 p.a. Yet if demonstration is an important part of the promotional plan so that television is necessary, then £60,000 -£70,000 is completely unrealistic for a national television campaign. The sum is wrong in absolute terms.

Possibly a solution is to interrelate the various factors affecting the marketing expenditure by quantifying them on the basis of assumptions even if these are subjective. Let us assume a market of £10 million which is not thought capable of much expansion, and which is traditionally conservative. The company believes it has found a product with an important advantage over the competition who spend in total about £900,000 p.a. and are estimated to be willing to increase this to some £1.2 million if a new entrant comes into the field. The new product lends itself to demonstration, so television would be most useful as an advertising medium in this case.

The company believe that they can obtain up to 15 per cent of the market in the first year with a considerable marketing effort, but how much should they spend? If the Nielsen ratio is applied, so that the company will need to spend at twice the average rate, the company will need to spend about £500,000, i.e. 30 per cent of £1.7 million which is the forecast of the total marketing expenditure in the market. Let us now apply the various weighting factors. The product advantage is considered very considerable – enough to justify a reduction of 25 per cent in the expenditure. The competition although established consists of sleepy companies who are unlikely to provide vigorous opposition, so a further discount factor of 5 per cent can be added. On the other hand the market has shown itself to be conservative and a real effort will be needed to induce the consumer to try the new product, so 10 per cent weighting is added on that score. Thus after the weighting factors are considered the expenditure comes down by 20 per cent to £400,000.

At the same time, the company needs to consider what level is necessary to make the required impact. The television campaign needs to be fairly strong nationally, so a sum of £250,000 would be by no means exaggerated for this purpose. About £100,000 will be necessary for a strong programme of below the line activity, including initial bonus, consumer promotions, and point of sale material. If some £20,000 is added for research the total comes to £370,000.

Against the above calculation a budget of £400,000 is very reasonable, and allows a reserve for flexible use during the first year. So, if £400,000 for the first year leads to the required profits on the project when incorporated in the profit and loss calculations, it can be adopted as the figure to be assessed further at the test marketing stage. Possibly the effects of £400,000 on marketing expenditure can be measured in the test market in comparison with another expenditure level in another area.

I am sorry if the reader is scandalised by such a haphazard approach to the establishment of an expenditure level which is often high and always important to the company. It is hoped that in time this will change and that there will be a wealth of data which can be used to decide on the right level of the marketing budget. At the moment, however, despite the claims of operational research and of simulation exercises, the marketing expenditure level for a new product is still a matter of personal judgement and intuition. Computer models can help in the calculations, but cannot replace personal judgement.

The marketing expenditure for a new product is very much affected by the company's investment policy. This governs the number of years which the company is prepared to wait before beginning to make a profit and then recovering its investment.

When companies were production-oriented, profits were usually considered on a short-term basis only. If a new product was not judged to contribute to the company's profits very quickly the project was shelved.

As companies became more aware of marketing considerations in the 1950s, the importance of long-term investment began to be appreciated. In fact it was generally recognised that it was not possible to launch a new product in a competitive market without a long-term investment policy allowing for a very strong and unprofitable launch to establish the product to a level at which the expenditure can be allowed to fall and a profitable position is reached. Thus pay-off plans lasting even five, six or seven years were thought acceptable for consumer goods and various new products were launched which represented a heavy burden on their companies' short-term profits.

Moreover they provided a serious problem in forecasting because what the company saw in the first year or two of national marketing and what could be verified in test market was a huge loss at a certain level of marketing expenditure. In theory the situation would change later, but just because the unprofitable forecasts were realised in practice there was no reason to have faith that the later forecasts of a change to a profitable position would follow. In fact a number of companies found that they could not diminish their marketing effort as planned because of the competitive position in the market and yet had gone so far that they did not want to abandon the project.

For example, a company could have been satisfied with the investment plan shown in Table 15.1. In theory, it is reasonable to assume a rise in share from 5 per cent to 13 per cent in the fifth year and, allowing for all the items of expenditure, a profit picture would result whereby the product would begin to run at a profit in the third year and

TABLE 15.1

Year	1	2	3	4	5
Market share	5%	8%	10%	12%	13%
Marketing expenditure, £000	250	200	150	150	150
Net profit before tax, £000	-80	-10	+50	+90	+110
Cumulative profit	-80	-90	-40	+50	+160

cumulatively in the fourth, so long as marketing expenditure falls from £250,000 in the first year to £150,000 in years 3, 4 and 5.

Yet if the company goes into a test market and obtains 5 per cent share with expenditure equivalent to £250,000, is this a good result? It fits in with the plan above, but the result does not provide the slightest reassurance that the share will go up to 13 per cent and that expenditure will drop to £150,000 by the fifth year. And these are crucial assumptions. If one or the other does not occur, the project is a disaster!

In the last two or three years, therefore, attitude towards long-term investment projects has changed. The most recent attitudes on investment by packaged goods companies in the UK were included in the survey that I conducted in May 1975 which was published in the *Financial Times* [15.3] (see page 60). Even if I do not believe that companies are as tough as suggested in the survey, it was noteworthy that 62 per cent claimed to require positive cash flow by year 2.

Respondents were clearly affected by the difficult economic situation of 1975, but I was still surprised and delighted that the majority had set themselves very tough targets requiring relatively little investment in the early years and so lessening the risk. It is now recognised that there are a number of factors against long-term investment, the main ones being as follows:

1 The rate of change in the environment and in technology is certainly increasing, so a product designed to satisfy specific consumer needs will surely die if these needs suddenly disappear or are radically changed.

2 In the very competitive situation which exists in most markets the lead achieved by any new product is very short-lived before it is copied by the competition. It is not surprising, therefore, that although old-established brands are often very vigorous and even growing after 50-60 years, the life of a new product is very short indeed.

3 There is little evidence that long-term investment policies have been particularly successful.

4 The high interest rates and unstable conditions of the 1970s have made early returns even more important.

There is a move, therefore, towards a compromise between the old production-oriented and the new marketing-oriented attitude to investment. The advantages of launching at an initially unprofitable rate in order to make the necessary impact on the consumer and the trade are still recognised, but there is reluctance to wait too long for the pay-off.

I am convinced that the latest attitudes are correct, because companies moved much too far into acceptance of long-term investment. It is easy to disregard the possibility of making profit even in the first year and yet this has been achieved by a number of recent new product successes.

If, therefore, the need to see the investment as early as possible is accepted, the company should try to begin making profit on a new product in the second year and certainly no later than in the third unless the opportunity is exceptional. The theoretical profit and loss forecasters, who delight in preparing long-term forecasts, showing very large profits after many years following great losses in the first four or five years, may scream at the need for early profits. There will be strong objections that in this way companies cannot maximise opportunities and that it will be impossible to launch any new product. There is certainly some validity in such objections, but on balance they must be outweighed by the advantages of the new attitude.

I am certain that companies must be far more concerned with the short-term profits of a new product if they are to lessen the risks and increase the chances of making money from new products – which must be the main object of the exercise.

The view which the company takes, therefore, of the new product's marketing expenditure at the beginning and in later years must be strongly connected with its desire to see early profit. It follows that the level of expenditure would be cut from that which would have been acceptable previously and even more attention than before will need to be devoted to the way in which the money is spent.

16 The role of advertising

The difference between good and bad advertising

The increasing need for a company to ensure that it is spending its marketing funds to best effect has already been pointed out and advertising is in general the most important single item in that expenditure.

It is also an item which is extraordinarily difficult to measure in isolation because of all the other variable factors affecting a new product's sales such as competitive activity, trade reactions, the sales force, display at the point of sale, etc. One is even tempted to conclude that it does not matter too much what the advertising is. So long as it is of average competence and is at the required level of expenditure, its effect will be relatively constant in helping to sell a certain volume of product in combination with the other forms of marketing expenditure.

Yet nothing could be further from the truth and those who believe that advertising has an average constant effect and no more can miss the opportunity of injecting an important advantage into the new product launch. For example, the advertising of Volkswagen in the United States is believed to have played an important part in establishing it there against the local competition. Again it is difficult to feel that Schweppes could have succeeded in the United States without the advertising which featured Commander Whitehead in his role of a typical English gentleman. Similarly the advertising must have played an important role in the success of such products as Guinness, Stork margarine and Fairy liquid.

An extraordinary example of the differences between advertising approaches is provided by advertising for a new dishwasher called Kim. In this case the product was sold direct to the consumer and so the advertising could be judged in isolation from any other factor on the basis of the number of coupons asking for a brochure, resulting directly out of the advertisement. Several advertisements were tested and in one case the same copy was used with two different layouts as illustrated in Plates I and II facing pages 148 and 149.

One would have expected, therefore, that there would be little or no difference in the response to the two advertisements. In practice, advertisement A (Plate I) pulled three times more enquiries than advertisement B (Plate II), an amazing performance which can only be attributed to the fact that the public must have found the design in A more pleasing or possibly more noticeable. If it is possible to have such a difference due to change of layout alone, it is feasible to imagine that good, well directed, advertising can benefit a new product to a remarkable extent in comparison with the effect of poor advertising.

Yet the difference between good and bad advertising need not be seen on the creative side alone. Differences in use of the actual media can be just as important. For example, it has been found time and time again that a company buying television time can buy even 15-20 per cent better than a competitor also using television who does not buy as effectively. This means that careful planning and buying can lead to a saving of £15,000-£20,000 on a budget of £100,000, or even of £100,000 on a budget of £500,000. These are savings which can make an important difference to the viability of a new product.

If it is accepted that the difference between good and bad advertising is an important factor in a new product launch and at times can represent the difference between new product failure and success, how does the company determine what is good advertising and what is bad advertising? The old cliché, quoting Lord Leverhulme's remark that half of advertising money is wasted, but one does not know which half, is too close to the truth for comfort even today. Yet the company must make every effort to try to finish up with the best possible advertising, for the rewards are high and so are the penalties for failure.

Because of the importance of advertising in the development of most consumer products, the company needs to choose the advertising agency to handle the product with great care.

At one time I was convinced of the need to call in advertising agencies very early on so that they could contribute more to a product's development than just advertising and media buying. This may still be the right approach in some cases, but not in general. Agencies have tended to reduce their services in the 1970s and to concentrate much more on the advertising of current products than on speculative new product work. Certainly my recent experience of agencies' work in meeting concepts at an early stage has been just horrible because of the lack of experience of the executives assigned to such projects. This has also been the experience of major consumer goods companies. There is thus some merit in considering new product specialists or creative consultants at an early stage, though I may be biased. Once the concept and product have gone through the evaluation stages, however, the right agency is vital in helping the company to implement the project correctly, implementation being even more important than the planning in the case of a new product, as I have already dared to suggest. A combination of outside creative consultants and independent media buying services is, of course, a possible alternative to an agency. Some companies have found this cost-effective and it is thus worth considering.

If advertising and the agency contribution are so important eventually, how should a company choose its agency? Very often there is no problem if the company already has an agency working on its existing products, as the new one is simply added to the others.

If, however, there is need to choose an agency – and a company already with an agency should consider the advantages of finding another one for the new product to encourage healthy competition – it is worth while drawing up criteria for selection. At the moment many companies, even large and experienced advertisers, are extremely subjective in this respect and tend to select a small number of agencies of good reputation whom they may ask to make a competitive presentation on the basis of which a decision is made.

This is indeed a strange procedure for choosing a business partner. While the company understands the importance of methodical market studies and research to find a market opportunity, it is prepared to give its advertising to an outside group on the strength of a presentation where there is often a premium on form over content, where the personality of one or two people can be the most important factor. And if the company appoints the agency, the people presenting may be never seen again by the company on a day-to-day basis because they are too busy working on behalf of other companies or presenting to prospective clients!

It seems reasonable that this important decision – the choice of an advertising agency – should be taken only after a systematic process of search and appraisal. I suggest the following procedure:

1 Establish company needs

Does the company only want creative work and media buying or does it want other agency services (marketing, market research, merchandising, pack design, etc.)?

2 Establish criteria for suitable agency

These should, of course, be in line with the company needs. The size of the agency also would need to be considered closely in relation to the likely advertising budget. For example, a budget of, say under £100,000 is unlikely to be very interesting to a large agency who, if it accepts it, will probably put its more junior executives on the account, while it could be one of the more important accounts in a small or medium-sized agency whose top management could well work on it on a day-to-day basis. Moreover it can be argued that a large established agency has much less incentive than a smaller 'hungry' one. On the other hand a company with a really large budget or one which requires very comprehensive agency services is unlikely to find what it wants in a small or medium agency. In fact it would be unfair to the latter to appoint it and become its dominant client, if there is a need to change to another agency six months later.

3 *Agency search*

Once the agency criteria are established, it may even be useful to prepare a screening system as for new products, weighting the various factors according to their importance. The company should then consider all the agencies according to the required criteria and it is thought that the large majority can be quickly eliminated mainly on the grounds of size, experience, facilities, or because they handle competitive products.

4 *Evaluation of short list*

A short list could be reached and, at a general meeting with each one on the short list, an impression should be formed once the agencies have the opportunity of discussing their past work and results for other companies and of showing the facilities which they can offer. The short list should become shorter as a result and then the company can do much by considering closely the other companies for whom the possible agencies are working and the advertising they are producing. It is always useful to discuss the agencies with one of their current clients who, after all, work with them on a day-to-day basis and so are ideally suited to assess them.

Finally, it would seem useful for the company to send one of its executives to spend a few days with the two or three most likely agencies. In this way he will see them at work for their clients and will be able to assess their faults as well as their good points in normal conditions rather than in the artificial situation of a special presentation which could be most misleading.

I believe that at this stage there should be enough information on which to base a rational decision. At the end of the line the company must choose the most suitable agency for its needs and the choice needs to be a good one. If it is not and if the company needs to make a change too soon, this is harmful to the company and its new product as well as to the agency concerned.

So the most suitable agency is chosen for the new product. The company must now ensure that the right relationship is established. After all, the agency is there to contribute professional expertise in advertising if nothing else, yet advertising is a field where everyone believes he is an expert and there is a strong temptation for companies to offend by dictating what the advertising should be. Sometimes the company will decide what advertising media should be bought against the advice of the agency's media buyer who may have been specialising in media buying for twenty years on behalf of hundreds of companies and who would be the only person really aware of all available media research data. The company can even go as far as to design press advertising layouts or prepare television videotape commercials and hand them over to the agency to complete.

If the company insists on being dictatorial, the advantages of having outside experts are nullified and the agency, even if it continues to work for the company in a slave-like manner, will certainly not be involved in the company's business, so its contribution will be minimal.

It is important, therefore, for the company to recognise the importance not only of advertising but also of the advertising agency and so to choose one which can be treated on equal terms. If the necessary amount of scope is given to the advertising specialists, they will try harder and the company will find a second body of people devoted to the success of the new product. For example, I know of a company which at one time did not even bother to check the advertisements before they went into the media. The managing director said to the agency 'After all, you know what we want to say to our market and you are the experts on how to say it, just go ahead and send me proofs for my files'. This attitude goes too far because the company abdicated its responsibility for final decisions, but it made the agency very conscious of its own responsibility and so the latter approached the advertising with a fantastic devotion, knowing that it was the final arbiter.

All the studies recently conducted in the USA and in the UK clearly show that the very large majority of advertisements are completely invisible to the public. We are bombarded by so many advertising messages during the day – on television, in the press, in the cinema, through the letter box, in the shops – that the chances of any one being seen and remembered by its desired market are extremely slim. It is vital, therefore, that the new product's advertising should be not only persuasive for its particular market but also distinctive, i.e. different enough from the competition to be noticed.

It is essential, therefore, for the agency and company together to hammer out a creative policy concentrating on a specific product advantage and not try to include all the virtues of the new product, so that at the end no single point registers.

For example, when Procter & Gamble launched their new liquid detergent – Fairy Liquid – it could easily have talked about a number of product attributes such as its washing performance, its value for money, its pleasant smell, its convenience, etc. Instead the decision was taken to concentrate all the advertising effort on the point that the product was kind to the housewife's hands, while its other attributes were taken for granted, and the constant repetition of the theme has made an important contribution to the product's success.

Similarly the same company's soap, Camay, obtained an important share of the fiercely competitive soap market through consistent emphasis on its high-priced French perfume. In the toothpaste market one new product would concentrate on decay prevention, another on the product's cleaning properties. In paint, the highly successful Magicote concentrated on the non-drip aspect, while the subsequent entrant, Crown Plus Two, promoted itself as 'a combination product', i.e. the only paint being both non-drip and hard and became the success story of the paint market.

It is necessary, therefore, to establish what are the factors in a new product which the consumer finds important and which would give it an edge over competition. Once this is established – and after all it should stem directly out of the new product development process – this most important selling point should form the foundation of the new product's advertising policy.

Until very recently the USA held a definite lead over the UK in the understanding of the need for such concentration on one point. Here, even if the point was established, companies and agencies tended to be nervous to concentrate on it alone and so cluttered the advertising with all the major points, in case any one were overlooked. As a result, nothing came across to the consumer.

Now, however, it seems that the situation has changed and the importance of this concentration on one point is recognised. Yet even then there is a gap to be bridged between a strongly concentrated policy and the appropriate creative execution. For example, if it is agreed to advertise a car on its manoeuvrability, it would weaken the advertising if it is found necessary also to include other points in the actual advertising, i.e. that it has much room in the interior or that it is very good quality or that it uses little petrol, etc. If one point is selected, it is normally worth while making a stark advertisement on the one point only. Such concentration is necessary to be noticed among all the advertising messages with which the consumer is being bombarded. Here is the way to more effective advertising.

Concentration of the advertising means that the correct selection of the particular selling point to be promoted is crucial. The initial concept search should serve to indicate the one or more selling points worth building the advertising on. Once the advertising has been prepared, it is normally advisable to validate it by pre-testing it.

Advertising pre-testing

If the advertising is important to the success of the new product, as it usually is in the case of consumer products, its impact and suitability should be checked before it appears.

Many companies are reluctant to carry out such research either because of the cost or because, in the pressure of events, there is no time to conduct it and change the advertising if necessary. Although in some cases this attitude is justified, more often than not the pre-test is not considered in relation to the total advertising appropriation. It does not seem reasonable to grudge the cost of pre-testing amounting to, say, £2000, if the advertising expenditure is £200,000 or £400,000. After all it is logical to assume that the pre-testing should improve the performance of the advertising by 1.0 or by 0.5 per cent respectively.

The actual form of the pre-testing does not matter too much. There are a number of approaches to this type of research which is recognised as one of the most problematical of all and there is no method which does not have some serious disadvantages. Yet, whatever method is used, it should enable the company to decide between two or more advertising campaigns.

Moreover, even if only one solution has emerged for pre-testing, the research will still be most useful, so long as there is enough time to change the advertising if necessary. It is also important for the company to pre-test all its new advertising if the results of research on one campaign only are to be interpreted usefully. A number of companies have accumulated a precious bank of information over the years using a constant research method. In this way a benchmark is available against which every new set of results can be assessed and the relative value of the new advertising can be determined.

Advertising expenditure

Advertising expenditure levels are obviously closely related to total marketing expenditures (see pages 149-57). Note that there has been a trend by consumer goods manufacturers to spend less on consumer advertising in relation to sales. Food has fallen from 0.97 per cent in 1970 to 0.74 per cent in 1975, drink and tobacco from 1.14 to 0.96 per cent, and toiletries, cosmetics and medical from 0.47 to 0.23 per cent [16.1]. Manufacturers' branding has suffered, as the retailers have become stronger and stronger and have forced the former to spend more on trade deals and trade promotion. This trend must be resisted within reason in the case of a new product – otherwise it will soon become another price commodity.

17 Testing and test marketing

The need for test marketing

If the preliminary research and all the financial evaluations look favourable, the company must obviously progress to the market place. In many cases there is no alternative to the national launch, particularly in the case of such products as durables, e.g. cars or washing machines, which usually require a decision on plant irrespective of the market area; thus the main risk decision is taken whether one goes into a town or a national market.

In packaged goods, however, traditionally it has been possible to go into an area. This is even truer currently, as in many cases it is possible for a large manufacturer to have his product made and packed by outside contractors, even if at a relatively uneconomic price, so that the decision on one's plant is not made until the product has been tested in the market place. Yet there has been, even in packaged goods, a trend against the use of area test markets because of the problems of prediction from a test market and the slowness of the process, while markets change more rapidly than ever before and it is necessary to take advantage of opportunities as quickly as possible. This view has been helped by use of other methods measuring repeat purchase such as the interesting technique developed by Unilever whereby a pre-selected sample of housewives have the opportunity to buy from mobile vans at regular intervals; thus it is possible to see what proportion of those who initially buy the product continue to do so. This has proved to be a most useful research technique which also has the advantage of security, as the products are not really sold in the market place; one must still accept, however, the artificiality of products not being sold in real shops and not being supported by real merchandising and advertising.

In my opinion the reaction against test marketing has been

 very much overdone. Whatever the problems of test marketing, the business of new product development is largely to cut down the risks and there is no better way of doing so than going into an area test market if practical. It is noteworthy that the more sophisticated marketing companies such as Unilever and Procter & Gamble have not wavered from use of test markets even though both have rightly been willing at times to chance their arm and launch a product nationally for practical reasons. Procter & Gamble in fact often put a product into test market and let it stay there for three, four or even five years, treating the exercise as a real laboratory in which they attempt to iron out all the bugs from a product before deciding whether to launch nationally or not. Thus Crest was tested in the Southern TV Area for many years in the early 1960s until Procter & Gamble decided to withdraw it from the UK because they did not feel that it had enough potential. The product came back into test market in the 1970s and to national launch in 1975 – an approach which may make other companies marvel, but which also shows the long-term approach and the use of test markets by such a professional company.

I make, therefore, no apologies for covering test marketing in some detail in the pages which follow, even if some marketing men may feel that test marketing has had its day. Most of them will probably change their minds after they have had a number of salutary failures resulting from too quick a national launch!

The place of test marketing in new product development

Test marketing is normally the last step in the development process before a new product is launched either in a large area or nationally and its role in the step-by-step development approach has already been mentioned briefly.

Whether it takes place at all or at what stage of the process must depend on the financial considerations. If the risk is small, it may be worth dispensing with it. Too often, however, companies make the mistake of proceeding too quickly to a test market as soon as a product is available, without fully realising that, by doing so, they are making a decision on the viability of the new product, by implying that it is worthy of the expenditure which a test market normally demands.

If the product can be imported or manufactured by another company, the costs of test marketing may not be great, but in most cases a pilot plant is necessary, there are disproportionate costs of research and of production of promotional material and the necessary marketing expenditure is incurred. The average loss per product during the test marketing as calculated by Buzzell and Nourse at $248,000 is an eye opener (see page 188), but even in the UK a sum of £50,000 or more for a test market is by no means unusual. The company should consider, moreover, the cost of using the sales force organisation in the area to launch the new product, to the detriment of the company's other products, and the risks of poor trade reaction if the product fails.

It is important, therefore, that unless there are special reasons against this policy, by the time the test marketing stage is reached, the product should have passed through enough stages to warrant the expenditure needed in a test market.

There are often strong pressures within the company either to rush through to test market or to dispense with it altogether. The main disadvantage is that it warns the competition and, if it is known that competitors are developing similar products or if it is very easy for them to imitate the new one, there is a strong temptation to launch nationally as quickly as possible and thus seek to acquire a lead over competition. This is obviously an important point and there are examples of companies indulging in leisurely test marketing only to be hammered by awake competitors being the first to launch similar products nationally. The success of Alberto Culver in the United States is at least partly attributed to such an opportunistic policy.

Yet it would be wrong to accept too great risks simply because of fear of competition. After all, if a company has settled on a step-by-step development approach culminating in a test market, this means that it has not accepted the risks of a national launch without a test market. Why should this risk be acceptable to the competition? And if the success or failure of the new product depends largely on a few months' lead, the project is surely not a very promising one. One of the factors which the company must have considered from the beginning of the project is competitive action and either the company regards itself superior in marketing terms to the competition or the product advantage it is planning to have will be substantial enough to produce profit for the new product over a number of years. In either case there is no need to panic and take unnecessary risks at the last fence. Even if the competitor decides to go first, this could be an advantage rather than a disadvantage. In practice I have found that rumours about competitive action are rife for years – even three of four years – before the competitor actually is ready and willing to move, so decisions on the basis of such rumours are most unwise.

The arguments for and against the test market must be settled on financial grounds. If the risks are high, it is usually worth while. Or if there is one or a number of factors to be tested (pricing, weights of marketing expenditure, distribution policies, etc.), which can never be satisfactorily researched except in the market place. If, on the other hand, the marketing costs are relatively low and the major expenditure on plant needs to be incurred before test market or if the product is supplied under licence by another manufacturer, the financial risk of national marketing is small, the risks being really incurred before the test market. In such circumstances there could well be a good argument for a launch in a large area or nationally without any delay in a test market area.

Pilot plant operation

The test market for a new product can be held to discover the answer to a number of questions such as:

1 Will the sales force be able to have the time to sell and merchandise the new product?
2 Are the distribution outlets selected the most suitable for the new product and will the trade provide the necessary support?
3 Will the company's organisation cope with the new product in terms of production, transport, servicing, etc.?
4 Is it more profitable to sell the product at £25 or £30?
5 Is it more profitable to have marketing support at the

rate of £100,000 ot of £200,000 nationally?

6 What market share, sales volume and finally profit are likely to be achieved nationally?

In practice a large number of questions such as the above are asked and many test markets are held to answer either one question or a combination of two or more. It is possible, however, to divide the main functions of a test market into two:

1 As a pilot plant operation.

2 To predict level of future performance on a national basis.

The pilot plant function is similar to that in engineering. It is assumed that, however much one plans, there will be unexpected snags in the final plant, so a pilot plant is built, not necessarily as a replica of the full-scale plant but as an approximation so that the engineer can see what the snags are likely to be in practice and can then experiment and decide on the best ways of solving them. Similarly in marketing there can be snags with a new product, particularly in the case of durables which usually have teething problems or if a company enters an unfamiliar field. It is unlikely that all the snags can be foreseen and eliminated in the preliminary planning, so the test market is held for this very purpose.

For example, a new company recently entered a consumer durable field in the UK and decided to sell direct to the public. The product was manufactured for them by another company and no experience of direct selling was available, so it was vital to start in an area where the company learnt, largely on an empirical basis, the best method of selling the product, while the organisation for manufacturing, delivering and servicing the product was perfected.

Another company had been selling over a long period solely through its own outlets and devised a range of new products to be marketed through outlets other than its own. A test market was held mainly to discover whether it was in fact feasible to obtain distribution in these other outlets over which it had no control.

Finally, a food company entering a new product field was concerned that there could be problems because the new product had shorter shelf life than the other company products. A test market took place, therefore, to see whether the new product could be handled by the existing sales force and distribution arrangements or whether special provisions would be necessary.

In cases where test markets are used for pilot plant purposes they work extremely well and are absolutely invaluable. In fact there is no other way to find the answers to many of the questions raised except in practice, i.e. under market conditions in a limited area.

Prediction problems

The majority of test markets, however, are held for predictive purposes and, even in a pilot plant operation, where the activity may bear no comparison with what would be done on a national basis, it is difficult to restrict the temptation of calculating the sales and projecting them nationally.

Yet, although there is so much anxiety to predict, there are also important problems in making such predictions. The reasons for these problems are well enough known:

1 There is no area really representative of the whole country. Each one has its own characteristics and companies and their markets have different strengths and weaknesses in different areas.

2 There are differences in the trade structure. In some areas the trade may be controlled by one or two local groups. In others trading organisations from outside the area are important and it may be difficult to obtain distribution in their outlets on a test area basis. In yet other areas the trade may be fragmented among a large number of small companies and businesses. Performance in one of these areas could well be different from what would happen nationally.

3 Competitive action is normally an important factor and there is no control over it. The competition can behave in one way in the test market and in another way on a national basis and this could be enough to make a considerable difference between the two situations.

4 The change in time between test market and national marketing could lead to differences caused by different seasonality, economic conditions, weather, etc. For example, a soft drinks test market prediction was com-

pletely wrong because of change in the weather which is of course an important factor in this market.

Points such as the above have been recognised for some time and enquiries have been carried out to see whether they in fact affect test market predictions to any degree. Studies in the United States have shown the lack of correlation in many cases between test market and national performance which could not be attributed to changes in a company's marketing policy following the lessons learnt in test market. Strong words have been used, such as '. . . traditional market testing has not lived up to its expectations when used as a predictive research tool. The time has come for us to do some serious large scale experimenting with new, and perhaps even dramatic, ways of making this tool more predictive' [17.1].

Such opinions were backed by opinion on both sides of the Atlantic. Jack Gold studied US retail audit data for seven established brands in six large areas and the differences between the areas were startling [17.2]. Assuming that each brand in each area were being test marketed, Gold projected the area sales in each case using three different projection methods, on the basis of the buying income of the population in the area, market shares and comparisons with the leading brands. It was then possible to compare the projections with the actual national sales as measured by the same retail audits and the conclusions were striking and disturbing. When one area projections were used, each area being at least 3 per cent of the United States, in 65 per cent of the projections the error was ±15 per cent and in 30 per cent of cases it was over ±35 per cent! When combinations of three areas were used for projection, i.e. at least 9 per cent of the United States, the results were more predictable, but even so the error was ±15 per cent in 40 per cent of cases. And 15 per cent could well be the margin between success and failure.

Similar analysis has been carried out in the UK [17.3] and again considerable area differences were found. Dr Treasure examined two brands. In one case he found that seven times out of fifteen the error was over ±15 per cent. In the other case it was ±15 per cent in fourteen projections out of fifteen. I have found similar results and in fact one projection I made was three times the actual figure!

It is not surprising, therefore, that in the last two or three years there have been serious doubts about the use of test markets for predictive purposes. The analyses of retail audit data compared projections and actual national sales at the same period of time, so what could the differences be between one year and the next? In fact the reason why test markets have continued to be used where possible was not because companies overcame the doubts but simply because no better alternatives were found.

A Nielsen study [17.4] has helped to provide more quantitative data on prediction; 141 test markets of packaged goods in the UK and the US were analysed. Of these, 77 went on to national marketing and so it was possible to compare market shares in test market and nationally. When the average national shares during the first year were compared with those in test markets, the results were as shown in Table 17.1. Thus in almost half the cases the test market share was within 10 per

TABLE 17.1

All brands launched (77 = 100%), %	Difference between national and test market share, %
28	±5
21	±6 - ±10
34	±11 - ±20
12	±21 - ±30
5	±31 - and over
100	

cent of the subsequent national performance, i.e. a share of 10 per cent could be assumed to be in the 9 per cent-11 per cent range in half the cases. No company could object to such error in prediction. However in 17 per cent of cases the error was over ±20 per cent, a margin which would probably be unacceptable. The question which needs to be asked is whether a company would view a margin of error of between ±10 and ±20 per cent as acceptable for test market projection. If it does, then, on the basis of the Nielsen study, this is likely to happen in over 80 per cent of cases.

A company should certainly build in a safety margin into its profit and loss forecasts and ideally projects should be sought with at least a 20 per cent safety margin. Nevertheless to allow the possibility of up to 20 per cent error for test market prediction alone, when there are so many other factors to be considered, e.g. cost of goods, sales costs, distribution, marketing expenditures, etc., seems high. In practice, I believe that few products can stand a difference of 20 per cent between test market and national performance, although the thought that in half the cases it need not be more than 10 per cent is certainly reassuring.

An approach to prediction

Whatever the hesitations about predicting test market results, it is obviously necessary to try and in practice good results have been achieved through meticulous planning of the test markets and careful interpretation of the results.

Having made the national marketing plan, it is advisable to prepare a national prediction model to be scaled down to the test area. It is not necessarily scaled down on the basis of population alone as it is important to weight the predictions according to the company's relative strength in the area, the regional pattern for the total market and for competitive brands, etc. Once all the factors are considered and weighted for the chosen test area, the prediction model, covering every period of measurement, could look as shown in Table 17.2. Such prediction models have a number of important advantages. The main ones are as follows:

1 Careful consideration of all the factors involved in the sales figure – and many more factors could be built in than shown above – must lead to more accurate sales forecasting than if one predicts sales levels only. For example, a sales forecast in a vacuum may seem reasonable until the likely distribution levels and the sales per shop stocking figures necessary to achieve the forecast are considered individually. It is then possible to see, comparing the prediction with the company's own previous experience and with competitive performance, just how reasonable the sales forecast really is.

TABLE 17.2

Period	Consumer awareness, %	Triers, %	Regular buyers, %	Shop distribution, %	Sales per shop stocking, s	Market shares, %	Consumer sales, £
1				19			
2	10	2.2	0.7	27	26	4	65,000
3	15	4.5	1.5	29	29	6	82,000
4	18	5.7	1.9	29	25	6	65,000
5	18	6.3	2.1	30	23	5	58,000
6	22	6.9	2.3	31	24	6	65,000
7	26	7.8	2.6	31	26	7	75,000

Moreover the more such prediction models a company makes and sees how they compare with actual results, the more accurate its predictions are likely to be.

2 If each department in the company is consulted on the prediction with which it is particularly concerned, e.g. the sales department on distribution, the advertising department on brand awareness, and the weighting factors provided by the departments are applied in each case, then there should not be any dispute as to the reasons why a test market is doing well or badly. The actual results compared with the predictions accepted in each case will make it clear where are the strong and the weak points in the test markets and there is much less room for argument than is normally the case.

3 The most important advantage stems out of the previous point, i.e. that it is known where the company is doing well and where badly. This means that there is no need to wait till the end of the test market to see what the final sales figures have been and then ponder whether the product is worth marketing in a wider area or not.

If detailed predictions are available for each period, say for every month, during the test market, then it should be possible to make appropriate decisions at an early stage. For example, if by the second month the distribution figures are well below forecast, it is probably worth stopping the test market until the distribution problem is remedied. Or if the proportion of consumers is very low, but, once they try the product, the proportion of them becoming regular users is above forecast, then it may be worth while changing the marketing activity to put emphasis on sampling methods in order to force trial of the product. Again the consumer side of the operation may be poor while distribution and stocks in the trade are good. In that case the consumer acceptance of the product should be reviewed as well as its communication and it may be advisable to stop the test market, change the advertising, and start again if there is nothing wrong with the product.

Thus the advantages of such a process as described above seem clear and work extremely well in practice. They enable the company to achieve above average accuracy in prediction and to use test marketing as a fluid and flexible tool, by treating it as a workshop situation in which it is possible to learn empirically the most profitable approach for the product.

Area selection

An important part of the process is the selection of the actual test area. Should it be a town, a series of towns, a television area or what?

All the US and UK evidence suggests that the larger the area the safer the prediction and it is now generally recognised that individual towns are not useful for predictive purposes. They are extremely suitable, on the other hand, for pilot plant operations, where the size of the area is not important. The only important factor is to have market conditions, whatever the area.

Towns are also used for test markets designed to provide blunt measurement of the relative performance of a particular factor. For example, it should be possible to see whether there is any broad difference in sales of the same product at different prices if it is sold in one town at, say 12p and in another at 15p. Or the presentation of the product could be tested in two different forms. Or it should be possible to measure the impact of different marketing expenditures, so long as the difference is substantial, say, at the national rate of £100,000 in one town and £250,000 in another well-matched town.

Finally towns can be used as a stepping stone to a larger area test market, in an attempt to minimise the risk of going on at once to a large area. The financial factors and the time involved must be the determining factors in this case, as the time span represented by first a town test and then an area test is likely to be well over a year for most product categories.

Some companies have attempted to use town test markets particularly as saturation tests, i.e. by spending in the test at a considerably higher rate than they could possibly afford nationally, in order to see what market expansion and penetration can be achieved. Such test markets are good in theory, but in practice they are almost impossible to interpret. For example, a company testing a new product in a very large market went into a town and spent at what would be an unaffordable rate nationally to discover that the product obtained an initial share of almost 20 per cent which declined over a number of months to under 10 per cent. As under 5 per cent would have been acceptable anyway, all the company could conclude was that by spending a great deal of money it obtained good results. It was impossible, however, to determine whether the test was good or bad as far as the product was concerned if backed by the planned appropriation nationally and I believe that most saturation tests must finish with such a quandary. It must be preferable to have a rate of expenditure in the area which can be related to national expenditure.

Area tests other than those in towns normally refer to television areas as served by the television contractors. It is rare for a company to consider the area tests in the same context as the town tests. Being much more expensive, they would not be used except for predictive purposes. These, however, are the most common, especially in the case of new products, so if there is a test market for a new product, it would be unusual if it were not held in a television area at some stage.

In theory test areas are selected on the basis of a number of factors such as:

1 Size.
2 Typicality of the consumer.
3 Media facilities.
4 Research services.
5 Typicality of the trade.

In practice, however, selection is normally a matter of elimination and the one or two towns or areas which are left with less negatives than the others are selected. For example, an area where the company is unusually weak or unusually strong is not good for predictive purposes. Then there are some areas where the company cannot obtain adequate distribution – a problem which is becoming more acute as the strength of multiple groups increases. Yet other areas could be rejected for various reasons such as:

1 The sales force are already engaged on other special activities in the area.
2 The area is poorly defined, e.g. the inhabitants shop outside as well as inside the area.
3 There are no suitable media.
4 The company has recently had a failure in the area

5 The market situation is completely atypical.
6 The area is too large.
7 It is so small that it would be dangerous to interpret the results.

Thus in most cases areas are chosen not because of their advantages but because the other areas have even more disadvantages or more serious ones. The various services and facilities which are provided by most of the television contractors and by some of the newspaper groups tend to be incidental and are taken for granted, though they are certainly useful once the area has been chosen.

Recently, several companies have used Channel TV successfully as a test area because it is feasible to obtain distribution, allow the use of TV and real shops and is completely discrete as an area [17.4].

Length of test market

The length of time which a test market needs to last depends very much on the object of the test market and on the market concerned. For example, a pilot plant operation could last only a month or two. For predictive purposes, however, it is normally necessary to wait long enough to be able to measure consumer repeat purchases and this can take a considerable time depending on the frequency of purchase in the market.

It is wrong, therefore, for a company to dictate that the test market must last, say, six weeks or three months if this is too short a time for repeat purchasing to take place, because the results of such a short test could be positively misleading. It is possible that in the initial period all sales are by initial triers and that the product is completely unacceptable so that no one returns. Yet, if not enough time is allowed for repeat purchasing, the test market could be interpreted as a great success on the basis of the initial sales.

The Nielsen study of 141 test markets in the US and the UK [17.5] covered the results achieved during each two monthly period and compared them with the results at the end of the test. It was found that the odds for correctly forecasting the final test results were only 1 in 9 after two months, 1 in 3 after four, 1 in 2 after six, 2 in 3 after eight and 5 in 6 after ten months. As the product categories referred to were all fast-moving packaged goods, the importance is underlined of having a test market for at least eight months and preferably longer if predictions are wanted from the test market.

In my experience, companies other than Procter & Gamble, do not spend enough time in a test area and failures occur that could be avoided if time were devoted to reading research reports, particularly repeat purchase data.

Research in the test market

A test market, particularly if conducted for predictive purposes, is by definition a research operation and so provision must obviously be made to obtain the necessary measurements in the area so that the company can interpret the results and have enough information to decide on its action during the test market and after its completion.

The above statement is self-evident, but in practice some companies object to a test market in which the research costs may be the most important single item. Yet wrong economy can and does mean that, having decided to spend, say, £3000 on research instead of the necessary £6000 on a test market costing the company, say, £40,000 altogether, the company just cannot interpret the results meaningfully because of lack of information and so the £40,000 is largely wasted.

The research should be linked closely to the prediction models and normally consists of measurement in two areas:

1 The consumer.
2 At the point of sale.

Retail audits to measure consumer sales are rarely enough, if they are not supplemented by consumer research into the rate of repeat purchasing. Without such information, the results would be completely misleading, as has already been mentioned.

Companies should also not neglect using their sales statistics to the full. Analysis of trade sales in total can be misleading if sales increase owing to the opening of new accounts and again a constant break out of repeat as against new orders is invaluable in establishing what is really happening in the test market.

18 International development

The world has now become so small in terms of communication; international companies span most countries; even the UK has stayed in the EEC following the 1975 Referendum; one can point a finger at such international brands as Coca Cola; all these arguments are often advanced, particularly by inexperienced people, to point to the need to develop products on an international basis. After all it is so insular for a US company operating in say ninety countries to consider the US market alone, while it is positively xenophobic for a UK or a French company to consider opportunities in its own country alone.

In some cases, particularly in heavy capital goods which are sold on a completely international basis, it must be right to think from the beginning about the international opportunities. In consumer goods, however, this rarely applies and all the international marketing experts, if there is such an animal, agree that international marketing is marked by strong differences between countries rather than similarities [18.1].

Even in the case of such an international product as petrol it is extremely difficult to have a uniform international marketing strategy as the large oil companies have indeed found [18.2]. Exactly the same is true of cigarettes [18.3]. If this is so in the case of an established product well known in every country, how much more difficult it must be to develop and launch a new international product!

In my experience it makes little sense to develop and launch new products internationally. If the vital task in evaluating and launching a new product is to cut down the risks, it must follow that to cut down on possible negatives in a number of different countries at once is either completely impossible or represents a sure recipe to introduce the lowest common denominator, i.e. a product which is so neutral that it will not attract any attention in any country!

I am convinced, therefore, that, if one were planning a new Coca Cola, it must be initially considered in the context of one country; once established in that country then it may well present opportunities in others, so long as there is scope to change it according to each country's needs. It is of course possible to seek concepts in one country for use in others and indeed I have been heavily involved in concept search sessions and concept development carried out in the UK for subsequent concept testing in such diverse countries as Spain, Germany and Sweden. Yet in each case the individual country's requirements were considered in the way in which the products were developed and presented and the research results varied greatly in each case.

Those who have a great deal of international development experience will agree, I am sure, with the need to take countries at a time on a step by step basis, using the kind of approach described in this book, subject to the amount of risk and of opportunity in each case. Those without the experience I implore not to listen to fine theories about international development and simultaneous launches in fifty countries. Let them take heart that even Unilever goes slowly step by step, country by country, and let them do the same. They will save their companies enormous sums of money, will not jeopardise their jobs and hopefully will launch products which will eventually become international brands.

19 Acquisitions and other external developments

Internal or external development

Once the company has spotted a market opportunity, it broadly has the following choices:

1 Internal development.
2 Licensing arrangements or other joint ventures with other companies, distribution arrangements, etc.
3 Acquisition.

This book has already dealt in some detail with the development of new products through internal sources of the company.

Licensing arrangements with another company are an alternative possibility and some companies have been most successful in obtaining profitable licenses, often from overseas, as the Rank Organisation with Xerox.

The most common alternative, however, to internal development is clearly acquisition of a suitable company; this method of diversification was very much in vogue in the 1960s both in the United States and in Europe.

In the US the success of such companies as International Telephone, Litton Industries and Ling Tempco-Vought, which have grown through a programme of constant acquisitions, has been imitated up to a point in the UK by, for example, Thomas Tilling and Cape Allman International. The realisation that the larger units have a considerable trading advantage has led to an unprecedented number of mergers and acquisitions in some surprising fields, e.g. banks and insurance as well as in cars, TV rental, electronics and food. Courtaulds, for example, claimed to have taken over 11 companies in 1967 alone and the pace hotted up subsequently.

The pace reflected the size as well as the number of bids in 1968. Mergers such as those between GEC and AEI, British Motor Holdings and Leyland, Radio Rentals and Thorn,

Allied Breweries and Showerings, Barclays and Martins Bank, Guardian and Royal Exchange Assurance, Westminster Bank and National Provincial, pushed into the second rank such mergers as that between Boots and Timothy Whites which in rationalising the total retail structure in the UK chemist trade would normally have been one of the more important commercial events in any one year.

The US companies were also very active, being forced by US anti-trust laws to seek expansion abroad rather than in the USA. Many of the largest US corporations have been extremely busy, especially on the Continent, in buying up local companies to obtain a foothold or consolidate their current business there and it was forecast that by 1982 US industry in Europe would be the world's greatest industrial power after the USA and Russia [19.1].

Within the United States acquisitions have presented probably the fastest method of growth for a large number of companies. For example, according to the Federal Trade Commission [19.2] the fifty largest food manufacturers in the US bought some 985 companies between 1950 and 1965, i.e. over one a year on average! According to the Commission the declining number of food manufacturers in the US and the fast-rising trend in diversification among the larger companies are closely related to this merger activity.

It is also noteworthy that, whereas at one time only a certain number of firms looked towards acquisition as a normal commercial technique, in recent years this attitude has spread to the majority of companies. Thus, as Louis Stern has pointed out [19.3], companies that in the past depended entirely on growth from within have ventured into the acquisition field, e.g. Hershey Chocolate which recently bought San Georgio Macaroni Company or Ralston-Purina which merged with Van Camp Sea Food Company in 1963. Similarly in Europe every type of company seems on the lookout for acquisitions either for offensive or for defensive purposes. For example, the French biscuit industry was highly fragmented among a large number of companies only a few years ago, but felt it necessary to merge into a small number of large units to combat the US companies entering the market. In the same way the biscuit market in the UK has become rationalised through mergers into two large groups – United

 Biscuits and Associated Biscuit Manufacturers – which between them dominate the market.

In recent years, however, the trend has changed considerably. Thus the value of actual takeovers in the UK fell from £2532 million in 1972 to £1304 million in 1973 and to £509 million in 1974. In 1975 it was as low as £291 million, but there has been more activity in 1976.

The difficult economic situation of 1974/5 has clearly been an important factor; the lack of companies to buy has been another; I have been involved in a number of acquisition studies in consumer goods markets where a list of several hundred companies immediately shows that they are either owned by some giant corporation or are tiny and not worth buying; even so the possibility of buying part of a company wanting to divest itself of unsuitable assets has emerged as a practical possibility, e.g. the acquisition of the Snappies business by Gillette from ICI in early 1975 or of Procea by Spillers from Cavenham in September 1975; possibly the most important reason for the fall in acquisition activity is the realisation that size is not everything, that acquisition is not necessarily the right path to development, that terrible mistakes have been made in the past, either through buying unsuitable companies or through paying too much. I even know a well-documented case of an acquisition made by one of the world's largest companies which actually bought the wrong company by mistake – it found out later that the acquired company was not operating in the chosen field of interest!

There is no question that companies have tended to pay too much for their acquisitions. In a competitive atmosphere of bids and counter-bids by different parties it is easy to feel that one must go on with the bidding above realistic levels. Even if there is no other bidder, companies have tended to exaggerate the estimated benefits of an acquisition. A study carried out in 1973 [19.4] based on detailed discussions with 30 out of the 50 largest British Companies showed that in most cases the new sources of earnings had failed to justify the cash and management time spent. The study also showed that 35 per cent of all acquisitions made in 1968-9 required a compound growth rate of 20 per cent or more p.a. for the next five years to justify a return of 10 per cent on the price paid.

It is ironic that merger and acquisition activity has declined sharply in 1974/5 because of the economic situation, whereas for the first time for many years a number of famous acquisition candidates may have become interested because of the very problems affecting investment and cash flow, while divestment opportunities, i.e. acquisitions of parts of companies are probably more likely now than before for the same reasons. Thus it is interesting that Cussons, having received inumerable approaches for many years, finally agreed to be acquired in early 1975, reflecting the problems facing a medium-sized company in an economic recession.

The advantages and disadvantages of acquiring a company instead of internal development need to be considered carefully and much will depend on the market concerned and on the developing company's attitude and organisation. The following factors should be considered in this context:

1 Experience of the market in which an opportunity has been found.
2 R&D experience of the above market.
3 Technical R&D facilities.
4 Time when profits are needed from project.
5 Liquid or share capital available for acquisition.
6 Existence of suitable companies to be acquired.
7 Balance between risk and opportunity of both internal development and acquisition.

If the company has the facilities and experience to develop from within, it is often more profitable to do so [19.5]. Even if the suitable experience is missing in many cases the company can easily recruit one or two individuals with the necessary skills and build the R&D effort round them. Such an attitude requires, however, senior and middle management to have a broad and flexible outlook towards marketing so that they are able to market successfully products in unfamiliar fields, especially in companies where management have been with the company for many years and so there is little experience of working in other companies and other fields.

Moreover, the cost as well as the time necessary for internal development of new methods should not be underestimated. An interesting study [19.6] in the US by Buzzell and Nourse on behalf of the Grocery Manufacturers of America calculated that in the period 1954-64 nineteen grocery manufacturers spent on average $94,000 per new product on product research and development and on marketing research before test marketing. During test marketing the average loss based on 72 new products was $248,000 per product and in addition capital plant investment, often substantial, needed to be added. If the products were launched broadscale, marketing expenditures per product averaged $1.4 million in the first year and $950,000 in the second, so that by the end of the third year only 61 per cent of the new products had broken even on a cumulative basis without allowance for the initial capital investment.

Although no equivalent figures are available for the UK, the US findings by Buzzell and Nourse certainly seem close to what needs to be spent on an important new product in the UK.

It is clear, therefore, that internal development can be expensive, risky and certainly takes time, although in the long term the opportunity is greater, if the product succeeds, than it would be through acquisition which would normally involve an already established product at a certain stage of market development. On the other hand acquisition seems safer as it concerns established products, but requires capital and often provides more modest growth opportunities.

In general it is unlikely that a company should consciously choose to grow either by acquisitions or internal development alone, whatever the market. Internal development tends to be a continuous process, certainly in the fields in which the company is already operating and in others in which it feels it can develop new products, whereas acquisition would be considered in specific cases, if there is a market opportunity which the company cannot exploit otherwise, if there is need to accelerate the company growth and capital is available and if there is a suitable company, or part of a company, to acquire, which fits in with the operation.

Dangers of acquisitions

There is no doubt that while in the United States the antitrust regulations make further mergers in many industries difficult, in Europe the trend for more and more mergers will continue once the economic situation improves. The breaking down of national frontiers within the Common Market and the recent increase in the number of countries within the Common Market will soon increasingly lead to an even greater realisation of the need of large industrial units to tackle what has become and will be the huge European market.

In the UK there was considerable pressure both in industry and in government towards further mergers, very much encouraged by the State-aided Industrial Re-organisation Corporation which has helped to bring about a number of mergers, including the GEC-AEI one and which actually canvassed the formation of large units to be a force in Europe. Neddy and various ministries also tried to stimulate mergers and it was noteworthy that at the beginning of 1968, Professor Blackett, President of the Royal Society and Deputy Chairman of the Ministry of Technology's Advisory Council on Technology, publicly praised the number of mergers which had suddenly developed and hoped that there would be even more.

A study [19.7] of 186 UK companies over the period 1954-63 shows that the largest companies are the most unprofitable. Those with assets of over £15 million, which means that they would be in the list of the largest 300 UK companies, had an average pre-tax return on assets of 14.6 per cent over the ten-year period. Companies with net assets between £1 million and £15 million earned an average of 16.4 per cent and those under £1 million 18.3 per cent.

It is dangerous, therefore, to represent mergers as the answer to every problem and so persuade a company's management that, if they have a problem or if they just want to grow, the automatic solution is a merger. It is easy to imagine that a company's management would decide that they must merge, whatever the circumstances, without thinking about the reasons for the merger, the characteristics of the other company or the subsequent circumstances. It is not surprising that Industrial Mergers state that almost 80 per cent of the 400 companies interested in acquisitions on their register have only vague policies or no policies at all for development.

It is vital, therefore, that companies should not yield to

such 'merger hysteria' which can lead to severe problems and to disasters. And there are clear indications that there have been a number of such failures both in the United States and in Europe as already mentioned.

Booz Allen and Hamilton analysed 120 US acquisitions in their 1965 new product study. They discovered that 64 per cent of the acquisitions were considered good, 25 per cent doubtful and 11 per cent had been sold again or liquidated subsequently. Thus over one third of the acquisitions were claimed to be poor or doubtful by executives in the acquiring companies, some of whom would be reluctant to admit that an acquisition had been disappointing. It can be safely assumed, therefore, that in reality well over a third, possibly about a half of the acquisitions had been either doubtful or failures.

It is noteworthy that the Booz Allen study suggests that companies learn from experience of acquisitions and that those which have made a number are more likely to be successful than those for whom this is an unusual occurrence. Thus 30 per cent of the companies which had made at least five acquisitions claimed that their last acquisition had been poor or doubtful, while the equivalent figure for companies who had made only one or two acquisitions was 46 per cent.

Why some mergers fail

It is difficult to classify a merger as a failure, as what seems a failure to the outsider could in fact be a success, according to the original criteria set for the operation. Moreover a merger which leads to poor results initially could prove most profitable in the long term.

Nevertheless the evidence already discussed clearly shows that many mergers do fail. Why?

There are many reasons, often depending on the companies or on the personalities involved when two companies decide to join forces. The main reasons, however, appear to be the following:

In the United States many companies go through a very thorough and lengthy planning process starting with a statement of objectives and going on to detailed examination of both markets and companies before a bid is normally made. Studies have clearly shown the importance of experience of acquisitions and companies without such experience should be even more insistent on thorough planning as a substitute for such experience.

After all, if it is accepted that a considerable amount of planning is necessary for a company to launch a new product, the same argument applies, only to a very much greater degree, in the coming together of two companies with different managements, personnel and procedures as well as with different products.

The financial implications of a merger are in fact normally considered with some care by the company and by its financial advisers and the terms are usually determined on the basis of a study of the balance sheets. Where many companies fail, however, is in consideration of the marketing implications of the merger. It seems natural that questions should be asked such as:

1 What is the market potential for the product range which is being added by the new company in relation to the existing range?

2 What happens if one sales force handles both companies' products or is it better for both sales organisations to continue?

3 What are the possible savings in distribution to the trade?

Yet such questions are often not studied in detail either because a decision needs to be made fast or because it is felt that to answer them it would be necessary to bring in a large number of executives with the resulting danger of a breach of security or simply because the importance of the marketing implications is just not appreciated.

It is not surprising, therefore, that a number of deals based on study of balance sheets alone turn out to be disastrous. For example, a number of acquisitions have taken place where a large company bought a much smaller one, the price being based on the assumption that the smaller company's sales could be increased substantially once they were handled by a large sales force. This can be a doubtful assumption and it has happened more than once that the smaller company's sales not only did not increase but in fact declined following the take-over, because products which had been vital to a small sales force became unimportant to a large sales force selling many high volume lines. In some cases it was also found subsequently that, even if there seemed scope to increase distribution, the small company's lines had in fact reached saturation in their outlets, e.g. it is absurd to consider that non-food products have potential for 100 per cent distribution in grocers.

One of the larger UK consumer goods companies made a very important acquisition recently and paid a high price mainly based on the assumption that the two companies had mostly the same customers in the trade and so very large savings in distribution costs would result. It was a reasonable assumption as the companies were both in the same type of outlet, yet what would have been a simple check of the two companies' records was not carried out and it was only after the takeover had taken place that it was realised that the assumption was not founded on fact. The two companies had unexpectedly little overlap in distribution and so the planned savings in transport did not materialise!

Another acquisition of a small regional company marketing short shelf-life foods within a small radius of its factory was made on the extraordinary basis that, following the takeover, marketing funds would be injected to expand the operation and that the profit picture would be projected in direct proportion to the geographical area covered. It did not take long to find out, after a handsome price had been paid for the company, that it was not possible to expand the geographical radius of what had been a very profitable operation when it covered a small area. Neither the products nor the organisation were suitable for a larger operation.

Many other fatal examples can be quoted – of companies which after takeover were found to market unacceptable products – of companies depending on one man who left after the takeover so that the companies collapsed immediately – of companies whose management had pushed up profits to the utmost immediately before selling and whose profit peak could not be maintained in the long term.

Yet what is self-evident, even if one talks from hindsight, is the ease with which many of the assumptions could have been checked beforehand and quickly. Very few companies seem to understand the importance of studying the marketing implications of a merger and their financial advisers, such as merchant banks, are rarely equipped to appreciate this problem.

2 *Little management capacity*

In some cases it is planned to integrate the two companies after the merger. In other cases the intention is to keep the two operations separate, the link being mainly a financial one. Quality of management is particularly sought, so that the company which has been taken over can continue to function as before under the same good management.

Yet it is largely a myth to suppose that the acquiring company's management, having negotiated the deal, can then continue to look after their existing company and simply wait for the money to roll in from the other one without spending any time on the management of the latter.

Experience of mergers on both sides of the Atlantic clearly shows the need for considerable management time after the merger as well as before it. It is unrealistic to believe that the company which has been taken over can carry on as if nothing had happened, as their management's incentives must have changed.

Either their management is so good that it is advisable to integrate it within the structure of both companies and it is not unusual for an executive of a company which has been taken over to emerge at the top of both companies eventually. Alternatively the acquired company's management is not up to the mark and so their role is partly or wholly replaced by the company taking over.

In either case the management of the latter needs to spend considerable time in directing the communication and integrating between the two companies and failures take place if management has not planned for this activity or does not have time to carry it out.

In the United States, experience of conglomerate mergers has shown that they can lead both to great failures and to great successes, though the latter can be temporary. The growth of Litton Industries and Ling Tempco-Vought was breathtaking, but at the same time this type of company seems particularly subject to great profit fluctuations as the problems of Litton Industries has shown. Litton became an empire covering manufacture and marketing of over 9000 different products and became involved in almost everything from space probes to typewriters and suffered serious profit problems. Ling Tempco-Vought exists no more!

The answer probably goes back to the principles of a conglomerate. It is essential to have a high stock market valuation in relation to earnings so that the company's assets can be used in taking over other companies with its highly-valued shares. The financial assets of the companies taken over can normally be rearranged then and the high price/earnings ratio has a snowballing effect on the acquisitions.

Thus the conglomerate operator bought fast and continuously – it is estimated that 70 per cent of all mergers in the United States in the period 1960-67 were conglomerates – and bought in unrelated industries on the assumption that good management methods apply whatever a company's field of operation, so that the same team can manage any type of company.

The above assumption is vital to the success of a conglomerate because the latter must depend on continuing success to hold its stock market image and thus be able to acquire more companies. Yet it is obvious that, although the same management methods can be adapted to many industries, each industry has its own expertise and it is unreasonable to expect one team to be as good in each industry as a good team experienced in that particular industry [19.8].

It is clear, therefore, that conglomerate mergers are particularly risky and the study by John Kitching certainly supports this view. If this is true of the United States, it is even more true of Europe where management techniques are on the whole less advanced and where there are very few companies really equipped to deal with the problems as well as with the opportunities of a conglomerate merger. Let me quote the President of Du Pont on the subject: 'Running a conglomerate is a job for management geniuses, not ordinary mortals like us at Du Pont.' One wonders whether it is even for geniuses.

Thus the dangers of a conglomerate merger are often not recognised and companies go ahead without appreciating what is really involved. It is hardly surprising, in the circumstances, if there are so many failures when a company, in addition to the normal problems of merging with another company, also has the task of dealing with completely unfamiliar markets and does not even appreciate the problems. The nearer the merger is to the company's experience, the safer the merger.

How to approach a merger

Although many mergers fail, a sense of balance needs to be preserved and the advantages in certain situations of considering a merger or an acquisition instead of internal development need to be borne in mind. It is vital, however, that the merger should be studied as an integral part of the company's development policy and not as a haphazard unrelated activity simply arising because a company may be available for buying. The acquisition should come as a result of a set development policy leading the company to specific market opportunities which are better exploited by acquisition than through internal development. At the same time flexibility needs to be preserved with any such process and an opportunity could arise if a company is suddenly found to be interested in a takeover. If this happens, the takeover simply needs to be related to the company's development policy and should be compared with the other possible opportunities facing it. Thus the two processes can be illustrated as in Figure 19.1.

Whichever the process, it is important to set out in advance the criteria required for the company to be taken over, which can be used as a basis for a screening system designed to differentiate between the various companies in the market. If the company is known to be available, it is still advisable to consider it in relation to the others as a better opportunity may present itself. If, on the other hand, it is necessary to find out what companies are available, it is worth while to do

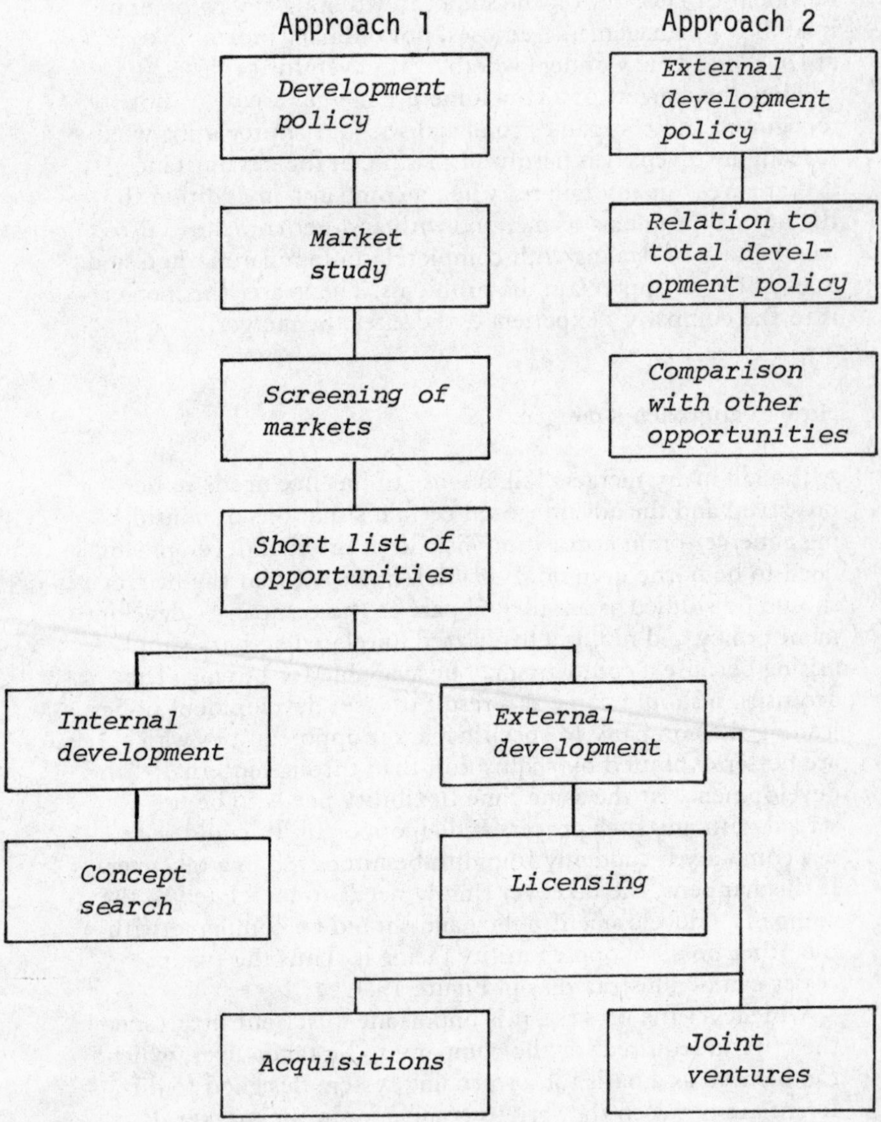
Approach 1
Approach 2
Development policy
External development policy
Market study
Relation to total development policy
Screening of markets
Comparison with other opportunities
Short list of opportunities
Internal development
External development
Concept search
Licensing
Acquisitions
Joint ventures

Figure 19.1

so at a relatively early stage, because time and money would be wasted if a very full study were carried out leading to perhaps one company which is then found to be uninterested or unavailable.

In practice it should be possible to make a short list of say 10-15 companies which look the most promising in relation to the required criteria and to approach them informally, in order to see whether they are interested or not in takeover in principle. Then, after eliminating those obviously not interested, the company can concentrate its attention on the others and finally decide on the most suitable one among them, with regard to both the financial and to the marketing implications.

The kind of process described above, relating the merger to a company's resources and policies, should cut down the number of failures and ensure that the mergers which take place are profitable ones. Such an approach is going to become particularly important because as the concentration of power in all consumer goods fields increases, so there will be fewer and fewer small and medium-sized companies. It is likely that the large majority of these companies will be taken over and so more and more often a company will be tempted to buy another one for no other reason than because it is the only one left in the field! Yet competition to buy the few companies left in particular markets is likely to benefit only the companies being taken over unless the decisions are taken analytically and not emotionally. The most successful companies will be those which will resist the temptation of taking over companies for the wrong reasons and which will see that, unless acquisition of another company can make an important contribution, internal development is likely to be a more profitable course.

Other forms of external development

Other forms of external development need to be considered as well as acquisitions. Joint ventures, particularly 50/50 companies, are fraught with problems. For example Brooke Bond Oxo and Ranks Hovis McDougall had a 50/50 company in the 1960s to persue joint development in the savoury snacks market, while Pergamon and British Printing Corporation also had a joint venture in publishing. Where there is no obvious directing authority, the dangers of failure are enormous; the risks are great enough in development when one company is in charge, but, where two are involved and there is no dominating partner, the chances of disaster are great indeed. Certainly both the savoury snacks and the publishing ventures mentioned above foundered completely, largely for this reason.

Licensing, however, must be of interest to technically based companies in particular and Rank Xerox is the obvious example, as mentioned. Even in 1975 Xerox provided all the profits of the Rank Organisation, despite the latter's diversification into hotels, catering, durables, etc.

Another possible route is that of the distribution agreement. For example, a US company looking at Europe may well feel that however large, it does not want to risk setting up its own organisation, at any rate for 5-10 years. The costs of large selling, distribution, administration and management resources are high and may not be justified, particularly if the success of the US products is uncertain. There are many examples of US companies coming into Europe, adopting their US tactics and finally going back to the States, their tail between their legs, following abject failure.

So there is much less risk and yet a chance of quick action and even early profit through a distribution arrangement with a suitable local company. Thus Pillsbury have been distributing their refrigerated doughs in the UK through first Unigate and then Kraft, while Wilkinson Sword started to sell in 1975 the Foster Grant range of sunglasses. The very long-term aspects of such an arrangement may be questioned, but, as a short-term method of generating turnover and even profit and of learning about a market quickly in real marketing conditions this is a method which is not considered often enough in my opinion.

20 Conclusions

It all sounds reasonable on paper, but does it work? The test of the approach towards new products and diversification as described in this book is whether a company adopting it is more successful than it would be otherwise.

I hope that my conviction has come through that the approach itself is not and cannot be a magic formula for success. There is no substitute for creative ideas. If these exist, however, it is most important that the company should have a policy and a set of procedures to sort out the most suitable ideas for the company and to progress them successfully.

Although there is usually a wide gulf in business between theory and practice, there is nothing in this book which is not already practised by a number of companies on both sides of the Atlantic. Unfortunately in the UK such companies are still few, many of them being US subsidiaries in this country. In my experience, the small group of companies with a disciplined approach to development and diversification, who are also not afraid to be flexible enough to learn from their mistakes and who regard decision and risk taking as normal business practice, are streaking ahead of the mass of UK companies who still find it hard to adapt their management attitudes and their organisation to this challenge. The next few years will show whether the latter companies will recognise their problems fully and so will change or whether they will be left behind and eventually probably become absorbed by the more successful ones.

In 1976 this kind of approach has been more widely recognised than before, but the theory needs first-class implemtation over many years to obtain a much higher chance of success. So few companies seem good at the implementation, however well they talk! I am still hopeful, however, that improvement will come.

References

Chapter 1

1.1 R. Leduc, *How to launch a new product,* Crosby, Lockwood (1966).

1.2 *New lamps for old*, J. Walter Thompson (1965).

1.3 E. Pessemier, *New product decisions – an analytical approach*, McGraw-Hill (1968).

1.4 P. M. Kraushar, 'New products – what is really happening', *Financial Times* (1 May 1975).

1.5 *The Nielsen Researcher* (Oxford Edition, May/June 1967).

1.6 T. Levitt, 'Marketing myopia', *Harvard Business Review* (July/August 1960).

1.7 T. Levitt, 'Market stretching', *Marketing* (June 1966).

1.8 W. Ramsey, *Financial Times* (12 April 1967).

1.9 *New products 1974*, Kraushar, Andrews & Eassie (1974).

1.10 J. Kitching, 'Why do mergers miscarry?', *Harvard Business Review* (November/December 1967).

Chapter 2

2.1 N. H. Borden, *The introduction of new products to supermarkets,* Doctoral thesis, Harvard Business School (December 1964).

2.2 D. S. Hopkins and E. L. Bailey, 'New product pressures', *National Conference Board Record* (June 1971).

2.3 *How to strengthen your product plan,* Nielsen (1966).

2.4 *New products in grocers,* Kraushar, Andrews & Eassie (March 1976).

2.5 E. A. Malling, *Marketing timing,* Management Research and Development Institute, Crotonville, NY.

2.6 *How to strengthen your product plan,* Nielsen (1966).

2.7 Mintel (May 1975).

2.8 'Brooke Bond to sell thrillers', *Financial Times* (20 June 1974).

Chapter 3

3.1 W. Ramsey, 'Product launches: the facts', *Financial Times* (12 April 1967).

3.2 S. King, *Developing new brands,* Pitman (1973).

Chapter 4

4.1 P. M. Kraushar, 'How companies organise themselves', *Financial Times* (15 May 1975).

4.2 Paper presented to Marketing Society Annual Conference (1973).

Chapter 5

5.1 H. Dougier, *European business* (France), (January 1968).

5.2 P. M. Kraushar, 'Organisation for corporate development', *Journal of Society for Long-range Planning* (June 1976).

Chapter 6

6.1 G. Cyriax, 'The case for being second', *Financial Times* (3 April 1968).

6.2 H. Ansoff and J. Stewart, 'Strategies for technically based business', *Harvard Business Review* (November/December 1967).

6.3 L. Adler, 'Time lag in new product development', *Journal of Marketing* (January 1966).

Chapter 8

8.1 P. M. Kraushar, 'New product research', paper presented to ESOMAR Annual Congress, Hamburg (September 1974).

Chapter 9

9.1 *Financial Times* (25 July and 1 August 1967).
9.2 J. Bittleson, 'Price is the only marketing tool left', paper presented to the Marketing Society (October 1975).

Chapter 10

10.1 A. P. Hichens, 'Rates and discounts', *Financial Times* (9 July 1968).
10.2 A. M. Alfred, *Discounted cash flow and corporate planning,* Woolwich Polytechnic (July 1974); *Investment appraisal,* HMSO (1967).
10.3 A. J. Merrett and A. Sykes: *The finance and analysis of capital profits,* Longmans (1963); *Capital budgeting and company finance,* Longmans (1966).
10.4 H. Bierman and S. Smidt, *The capital budgeting decision,* Macmillan, NY (1960).
10.5 B. G. Bodroghy, 'Risk and return and DCF', *The Director* (July 1966).
10.6 G. R. Conrad and I. H. Plotkin, 'Risk/return: US industry pattern', *Harvard Business Review* (March/April 1968).

Chapter 12

12.1 Bill Darden, 'An operational approach to product pricing', *Journal of Marketing* (April 1968).
12.2 A. R. Oxenfeldt, *Pricing for marketing executives,* Wadsworth (1961).
12.3 A. Gabor, C. Granger and A. Sowter, 'Foundations of market-oriented pricing: the attitude of the consumer to prices', paper presented to a Symposium on Pricing, University of Bradford Management Centre (January 1967

12.4 A. Gabor and C. Granger, 'On the price consciousness of consumers', *Journal of the Royal Statistical Society*, Series C, Volume X, Number 3 (1961).

12.5 A. Sowter and P. M. Kraushar, 'Pricing research', paper presented to the Market Research Society Annual Conference (1972).

12.6 A. Sowter, A. Gabor and C. Granger, 'The effect of price on choice: a theoretical and empirical investigation', *Applied Exonomics* (1971).

12.7 A. Sowter and A. Billson, 'Practical problems in buy response', paper presented to the Social Science Research Council Conference (April 1975).

12.8 A. Gabor, *Principles and practices,* Heineman (1977).

12.9 A. Bergfeld, J. Earley and W. Knoblock, *Pricing for profit and growth,* Prentice-Hall (1962).

Chapter 13

13.1 P. M. Kraushar, paper presented to ESOMAR Annual Congress, Hamburg (1974).

13.2 L. A. Parker, address to PERA (June 1968).

13.3 A. Leyshon, 'Product testing in the automative industry', *Journal of the Market Research Society* (April 1968).

13.4 S. King, *Developing new brands,* Pitman (1973).

Chapter 14

14.1 N. H. Borden, 'The introduction of new products to supermarkets, Doctoral thesis, *Harvard Business School* (December 1964).

14.2 Institute of Grocery Distribution/Nielsen Conference on Stock-cutting in Grocers (1975).

14.3 *New products in the grocery trade,* Kraushar, Andrews & Eassie (April 1970, July 1971, January 1974, March 1976).

14.4 *New product review,* Mintel (1975).

15.1 *Setting advertising appropriations,* Marketing Society (1967).
15.2 *Nielsen Researcher* (January/February 1964).
15.3 P. M. Kraushar, 'New products – what is really happening?, *Financial Times* (May 1975).

Chapter 16

16.1 D. Dunbar, paper presented to ADMAP Conference, Madrid (October 1976).

Chapter 17

17.1 A. Achenbaum, address to American Marketing Association (1964).
17.2 J. Gold, 'Testing test market predictions', *Journal of Marketing Research* (August 1964).
17.3 J. Treasure, address to Marketing Society (1964); P. M. Kraushar, 'Some aspects of test marketing', *Advertiser's Weekly* (15 June 1966).
17.4 R. W. F. Eassie, 'Testing the potential of Channel', *Adweek* (6 June 1975).
17.5 *Nielsen Researcher* (January/February 1968).

Chapter 18

18.1 'Is the world one market', paper presented to the Marketing Society Annual Conference (1967).
18.2 Marketing Society International Group Meeting (March 1975).
18.3 K. Mann, address to the Marketing Society (1973).

Chapter 19

19.1 J. J. Servan-Schreiber, *The American challenge,* Hamish Hamilton (1968).

19.2 *The structure of food manufacturing,* Technical Study No. 8, US Government Printing Office (1966).
19.3 L. W. Stern, 'Acquisitions: another viewpoint', *Journal of Marketing* (July 1967).
19.4 'Planning research and systems', *Financial Times* (1973).
19.5 'Growth from within may pay off faster', *Business Week* (17 September 1966).
19.6 R. D. Buzzell and R. E. M. Nourse, *Product innovation: the product life cycle and competitive behaviour in selected food processing industries,* Arthur D. Little (1966).
19.7 J. M. Samuels and D. Smyth, *Economia* (June 1968).
19.8 'The perils of the multi-market corporation', *Fortune* (February 1967).

Index